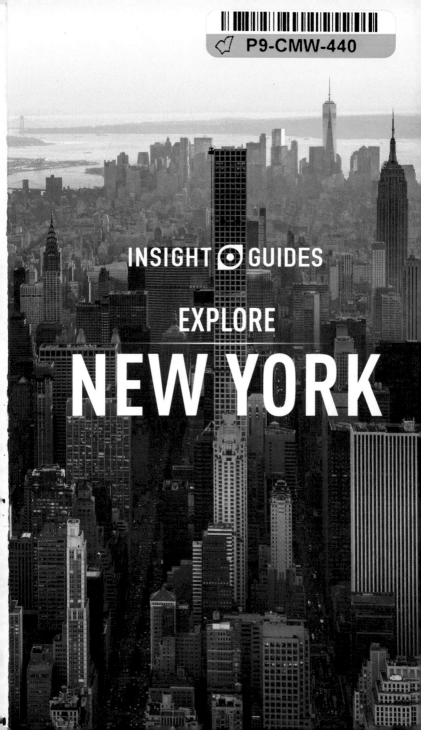

INSIGHT ◉ GUIDES

EXPLORE

NEW YORK

PLAN & BOOK
YOUR TAILOR-MADE TRIP

BRAZIL **CHILE** **ECUADOR**

TAILOR-MADE TRIPS & UNIQUE EXPERIENCES CREATED BY LOCAL TRAVEL EXPERTS AT INSIGHTGUIDES.COM/HOLIDAYS

Insight Guides has been inspiring travellers with high-quality travel content for over 45 years. As well as our popular guidebooks, we now offer the opportunity to book tailor-made private trips completely personalised to your needs and interests.
By connecting with one of our local experts, you will directly benefit from their expertise and local know-how, helping you create memories that will last a lifetime.

HOW INSIGHTGUIDES.COM/HOLIDAYS WORKS

STEP 1

Pick your dream destination and submit an enquiry, or modify an existing itinerary if you prefer.

STEP 2

Fill in a short form, sharing details of your travel plans and preferences with a local expert.

STEP 3

Your local expert will create your personalised itinerary, which you can amend until you are completely satisfied.

STEP 4

Book securely online. Pack your bags and enjoy your holiday! Your local expert will be available to answer questions during your trip.

BENEFITS OF PLANNING & BOOKING AT INSIGHTGUIDES.COM/HOLIDAYS

PLANNED BY LOCAL EXPERTS
The Insight Guides local experts are hand-picked, based on their experience in the travel industry and their impeccable standards of customer service.

SAVE TIME & MONEY
When a local expert plans your trip, you save time and money when you book, even during high season. You won't be charged for using a credit card either.

TAILOR-MADE TRIPS
Book with Insight Guides, and you will be in complete control of the planning process, from the initial selections to amending your final itinerary.

BOOK & TRAVEL STRESS-FREE
Enjoy stress-free travel when you use the Insight Guides secure online booking platform. All bookings come with a money-back guarantee.

WHAT OTHER TRAVELLERS THINK ABOUT TRIPS BOOKED AT INSIGHTGUIDES.COM/HOLIDAYS

Trip to Portugal

Every step of the planning process and the trip itself was effortless and exceptional. Our special interests, preferences and requests were accommodated resulting in a trip that exceeded our expectations.

Corinne, USA ★★★★★

Trip to Vietnam

The organization was superb, the drivers professional, and accommodation quite comfortable. I was well taken care of! My thanks to your colleagues who helped make my trip to Vietnam such a great experience.

Heather ★★★★★

CONTENTS

ART ENTHUSIASTS

There's more art than can be seen in a lifetime: from the big five – the Met (route 6), MoMA (route 3), Whitney (route 12), Guggenheim, and Frick (route 7) – to Chelsea's gallery scene (route 11).

RECOMMENDED ROUTES FOR...

FOODIES

For fresh produce try Union Square Greenmarket, Eataly, or Chelsea Market (route 11), while Dean & Deluca (route 13) and Katz's Delicatessen (route 14) are packed with gourmet goodies.

MOVIE BUFFS' NEW YORK

King Kong clambered up the Empire State Building (route 1); Holly Golightly breakfasted at Tiffany's (route 1); Travis Bickle wandered Times Square (route 2); and the Corleones caused big trouble in Little Italy (route 14).

NIGHTLIFE

Check out the alt-rock scene on the Lower East Side (route 14); catch a set at a Greenwich Village jazz club (route 12) or Harlem's Apollo (route 9); or dance all night at a Meatpacking District hotspot (route 12).

THE PERFORMING ARTS

Take in a Broadway show on the Great White Way (route 2); the ballet at Lincoln Center (route 8); an off-Broadway romp in the East Village (route 14); or free Shakespeare in Central Park (route 5).

SHOPPERS

Go on a shopping spree at Fifth Avenue department stores (route 1); visit boutiques in Soho (route 13) and the Meatpacking District (route 12); or browse 18 miles of books at the Strand Book Store (route 12).

SKYSCRAPER SPOTTING

Explore the vertical city, including the Flatiron (route 11), the Art Deco-era Chrysler (route 4), and Empire State (route 1) buildings, along with high-rise Lower Manhattan (route 15).

SPECTACULAR VIEWS

Take in glorious views from the Empire State Building (route 1), Top of the Rock at Rockefeller Center (route 1), Brooklyn Bridge (route 17), Statue of Liberty (route 16), or Staten Island Ferry (route 16).

INTRODUCTION

An introduction to New York's geography, customs and culture, plus illuminating background information on cuisine, history and what to do when you're there.

Fifth Avenue at night

EXPLORE NEW YORK

The 62 million-plus visitors who come each year arrive with skyscraper-high expectations, but with jaw-dropping architecture, world-class cultural sights, and fabulous shops and restaurants, the Big Apple does not disappoint.

In his writings on the city, *Here is New York*, the children's author, critic, and Pulitzer Prize-winner E.B. White wrote, 'New York is nothing like Paris; it is nothing like London; and it is not Spokane multiplied by sixty, or Detroit multiplied by four. It is by all odds the loftiest of cities. It even managed to reach the highest point in the sky at the lowest moment of the Depression.'

Since its purchase by the Dutch in 1626, through its growth as a maritime hub, to its contemporary position as the cultural and financial center of the United States, New York his risen to become a crossroads of the world and a place where the air tingles with the promise that everything is possible.

Statistics

The statistics are quite something: 6,400 miles (10,300km) of streets, 578 miles (930km) of waterfront, 26,000 restaurants, around 13,000 yellow taxis, almost 6,000 city buses, 150 museums, and 400 art galleries, more than 240 theaters, and 30,000 acres (11,736 hectares) of parks and beaches. Whatever you're after, from world-class museums on the Upper East Side to cutting-edge couture in the Meatpacking District, you'll find it here. If you stay in a sky-high hotel far above the teeming streets, or stroll in Central Park, or walk out onto the terrace overlooking the Hudson River at the Cloisters, you may even be able to find that city-center rarity: peace and quiet.

THE BOROUGHS

New York City covers a surface area of 302 sq miles (782 sq km), and is divided into five boroughs: Manhattan, Brooklyn, Queens, the Bronx, and Staten Island. Manhattan, the smallest borough, has a surface area of almost 23 sq miles (59 sq km), but is the most densely populated part of the city.

It remains open to debate how New York got its 'Big Apple' tag. Some say that the nickname came from a 1920s newspaper column about horse racing called 'Around the Big Apple.' Others say it was used by jazz players to indicate getting to the top of their profession, or reaching 'the Big Apple.'

Statue of Liberty   *Downtown Manhattan from the Brooklyn Bridge*

NEW YORKERS

Population and melting pot

According to the US Census Bureau, New York City has a population of 8.6 million. Of that figure, approximately 1.7 million people reside in Manhattan, 2.65 million in Brooklyn, 2.4 million in Queens, 1.5 million in the Bronx, and around 480,000 in Staten Island.

Although there are other cities in the United States with a high percentage of foreign-born residents, none can match the range or diversity of the ethnic communities of New York. Here,

Posing for pictures on the Brooklyn Bridge

around 32 percent of inhabitants are of European descent, 24 percent are African-American or African-Caribbean, 29 percent are Hispanic, and 14 percent are Asian. A former mayor, David Dinkins, once described the city as a 'gorgeous mosaic.'

The classic New Yorker

New Yorkers are stereotypically portrayed as being as relentlessly energetic as their hometown is fast-paced. Frenetic or not, this energy is perhaps what gives New Yorkers their edge and makes them so sure that Manhattan is the center of the universe. Increasing numbers are choosing to retire in the city, lured by the ease of getting around and the many attractions.

Resilience is also a key attribute. The reaction of most city inhabitants to the attacks of September 11, 2001, when terrorists crashed two hijacked jets into the towering World Trade Center, or more recently when Hurricane Sandy caused havoc in Lower Manhattan, was to respond with characteristic resolve to recover and rebuild.

CLIMATE

New York is blessed with sunshine year-round, but it has four distinct seasons. Summers can be steamy, with temperatures as high as 96°F (36°C), and winter days may dip as low as 9°F (-13°C). Happily, extreme heat or cold spells are usually brief; typical summer day tem-

Greenwich's White Horse Tavern

peratures are around 85°F (29°C) and winters in the 30–45°F (-1–7°C) range. Snowfalls are generally light, though every few years a major storm blankets the city, which thrills cross-country skiers, who head for Central Park. April brings showers, but May and June can be delightful, and the bright fall weather in September and October makes this the ideal time to visit. Spring and fall days average 60–75°F (15–24°C).

WATERWAYS

New York lies at the mouth of the Hudson River, which borders Manhattan's West Side. On the other side, the East River, separating Manhattan from Brooklyn and Queens, is a narrow strip of water linking Long Island Sound and Upper New York Bay. The southern portions of Brooklyn and Queens have sandy shores on the Atlantic Ocean. It is estimated that it takes strong swimmers an average of seven hours and 15 minutes to swim around Manhattan (not recommended).

A WALKERS' CITY

Unlike many cities in the United States, New York is a great place for walkers, helped by the fact that for the most part it is organized on a straightforward grid plan – numbered streets (north–south) and avenues (east–west). Pay little heed to the fancied-up Avenue of the Americas tag for good old Sixth Avenue, but watch out for the crazy-quilt pattern below 14th Street.

The West Village has streets unique to its neighborhood, many running at odd angles, which makes navigating this area a fun challenge even for long-time New Yorkers. Things really change south of Houston Street, where the numbered streets end altogether. Keep in mind that Fifth Avenue and, to the north, Central Park, mark the division between east and west.

Staying safe

Some people fear walking around New York because of supposed pickpockets or would-be attackers, but in fact the

---

Urban woodland

When Henry Hudson sailed up the river that bears his name, his first mate, Robert Juett, wrote: 'We found a land full of great tall oaks, with grass and flowers, as pleasant as ever has been seen.' New York still has over 28,000 acres (11,300 hectares) of parks, of which 10,000 acres (4,000 hectares) are wooded. Peregrine falcons nest on Midtown skyscraper ledges, and coyotes occasionally prowl from Westchester County down into the Bronx. Frederick Law Olmsted, the architect who laid out Central Park, wrote that, 'the contemplation of natural scenes… is favorable to the health and vigor of men.'

Busy streets   *In Little Italy*

city has been one of America's safest large cities for years. Such crime that does occur tends to be as random in nature as absolutely anywhere else in the world, and, as elsewhere, ostentatious displays of jewelry or wealth tend to invite unwanted attention.

Since New York is generally a lively place at all hours, there are only a few locations you should avoid. Most streets are consistently populated – although Midtown and southern Manhattan business areas are more deserted in the evenings, when the East and West Villages and Theatre District are hopping. Central Park, Battery Park, and Harlem are best avoided after dark.

DON'T LEAVE NEW YORK WITHOUT...

Taking in a view of the city skyline. Whether you ascend the Empire State Building for a panoramic view, lie back in Central Park looking up at the forest of buildings, or cross the Brooklyn Bridge for an unimpeded look at Lower Manhattan's skyline, be sure to find a place to survey what is possibly the world's greatest urban landscape. See page 28, page 48, and page 98.

Sailing to see the Statue of Liberty. Hop aboard a direct ferry (which also goes on to Ellis Island) or grab a free ride on the Staten Island Ferry to get a prime view of Lady Liberty. See page 97.

Paying a visit to MoMA. With one of the most incredible collections of modern art in the world, including works by Picasso, Warhol, and Van Gogh, housed in a purpose-built gallery that is remarkable in and of itself, MoMA is unmissable. See page 38.

A walk along the High Line. Climb one of its many entrance stairways to quickly escape the hurried crowds and metallic roars of the city. The path, lined with native flora and wooden benches, is ideal for wiling away an hour or for a relaxed stroll between Chelsea and the Meatpacking District. See page 82.

Stocking up on local eats. Visit local institution Zabar's, in the Upper West Side, chow down on a streetside hot dog, or explore the Lower East Side's range of traditional Jewish foods. See page 64 and page 90.

Giving your regards to Broadway. Even if you can't get tickets to a show, spend some time among the bright lights of the Great White Way, perhaps stopping for a deli lunch amidst portraits of famous theatrical folk. See page 34.

Crossing the Brooklyn Bridge. Marvel at the incredible 19th-century engineering as you cross this iconic bridge, which leads to the ever-increasingly hip borough of Brooklyn. See page 98.

Getting out at night. Whether it's hearing jazz in a classic Greenwich joint or cocktails in an achingly hip Meatpacking District bar, find out why New York's earned a reputation as the city that never sleeps. See page 122.

Times Square draws in the crowds

SUBWAYS, BUSES, AND TAXIS

In addition to the city being so straightforward to navigate on foot, it also has excellent subway and bus systems. You can sometimes find paper maps at subway stations and on buses, but there are also excellent transportation apps for most smartphones. Despite reports to the contrary, subways are considered fairly clean and safe – although it's still best to avoid traveling on your own after 11pm. The subway is usually the fastest way of getting around, especially for long distances, although walking is generally quicker if you're only traveling a few blocks.

Buses are useful and, while very slow, may seem less intimidating than navigating the subway. They are best for traveling cross-town (east-west) and can be a cheap way to see the sights. Each bus has a digital destination sign, and route maps are posted at every stop.

Those iconic yellow taxis are easy to become dependent on – unlike many cities, where you have to arrange for taxis in advance, in New York they just seem to appear (except when it's raining) and can be hailed anywhere you spot the light signifying the cab is available. New York car taxis date from 1907, when Harry N. Allen founded the New York Taxicab Company; he chose yellow after reading a study that said it was the easiest color to spot. Cab fares can mount up fast. Note that if you're trying to get somewhere at rush hour, it can be a long, frustrating, and expensive ride, and it's probably a better idea to catch the subway. As is the case in big cities across the world, taxi apps have changed the game, and Uber and Lyft cars now outnumber traditional yellow taxis by 4 to 1 in New York City.

An exceptional city

By the end of their first trip to New York, most visitors are hooked. Nothing is quite as exhilarating as walking between the skyscrapers of Midtown for the first time, seeing the iconic Statue of Liberty looming over you from the ferry dock, or even just strolling through Central Park on a sunny day or a blustery winter afternoon. Remember to walk purposefully and you'll fit right in. You'll soon discover why New Yorkers have a right to feel that there's no place quite like their home.

Taxis and The Shops at Columbus Circle

Battery Park – tourist souvenirs

TOP TIPS FOR EXPLORING NEW YORK

Reservations. Unless you plan to eat at a diner or cafeteria, be sure to call ahead and book, especially for hot new spots. And even if you have 'resos,' don't be surprised if you still have to wait a while to be seated. The only surefire way of beating the crowds is to eat at off-hours.

Apple Store. You can surf the web and check your email (for free) at New York's flagship Apple Store on any one of the computers on display 24 hours a day, 365 days a year.

Cheap tickets. Discount tickets for same-day shows can be purchased at the TKTS booth on Duffy Square. Evening tickets: Mon–Sat 3–8pm, Tue 2–8pm, Sun 3–7pm; matinee tickets: Wed, Thu, Sat 10am–2pm, Sun 11am–3pm; cash or credit cards accepted.

Joint tickets and talks. CityPASS tickets are available from Top of the Rock which also give entry to the American Museum of Natural History, Met, Statue of Liberty, Ellis Island, and 9/11 Memorial & Museum. Free gallery talks at MoMA are offered daily (except Tuesdays) at 11.30am and 1.30pm. Family tours and workshops are available, too, with programs designed especially for children.

Bike lane. Upper West-siders can now go faster (and safer) by bike with the bike lane on Columbus Avenue that runs from W 109th Street to W 69th Street (a New York City Cycling Map is available at www.nyc.gov). Alternatively, cycle through Central Park, which went completely car-free in 2018. Bike rentals are available at

1391 Sixth Avenue, (tel: 212-664-9600; www.bikerentalcentralpark.com).

Harlem guided tours. Harlem Spirituals (tel: 212-391-0900; www.harlemspirituals.com) and Harlem Heritage Tours (tel: 212-280-7888; www.harlemheritage.com) offer some of the best guided tours in the district, with themes such as heritage and history, gospel on Sundays, and evening jazz excursions.

Medieval music. Call 212-923-3700 or go to www.metmuseum.org/visit/visit-the-cloisters for information about concerts at The Cloisters. Performances are held in the 12th-century Fuentidueña Chapel and feature medieval compositions played on period instruments. Concert ticket prices include free same-day admission to the museum.

Governors Island. Once a major US military base, this is now 172 acres (70 hectares) of parkland offering walking and biking trails, historic forts and buildings, picnicking and peerless views. Free 10-minute ferry rides from the Maritime Terminal near Battery Park Mon–Fri 10am–4.15pm, Sat–Sun 10am–5.30pm from early May–late October (www.govisland.com).

Long Island beaches. Although New York lies on the coast, the beaches accessible by subway tend to be crowded, especially on hot summer weekends. The nicest are two to three hours by train or bus from Manhattan, on Long Island or in New Jersey.

Striped bass at Daniel

FOOD AND DRINK

Visitors will quickly discover why New Yorkers are passionate about food. The city boasts an amazing variety of delicious choices from haute cuisine to street carts, with prices to match.

New York has always had a reputation as a culinary melting pot. From Jewish delicatessens to Mexican taco joints to a vast market full of Italian eateries, people can enjoy a staggering range of food at every price point – they can order a $2 hot dog or a $52 hamburger. Diners are a New York institution found in almost every neighborhood, serving from breakfast through dinner with a wide variety of choices from snacks, sandwiches, and salads to full meals, all at moderate prices. The city's top-drawer restaurants take pride in serving the very best of French, Italian, Asian, and New American cuisine.

FASHIONS IN FOOD

Fashions are vital in New York, and the contemporary trend is for famous-name kitchens fronted by celebrity chefs, both homegrown and from as far afield as London, Paris, and Italy. Current stars include Jean-Georges Vongerichten, David Chang, and April Bloomfield.

Another current fashion is to preface food styles by the words 'haute' and 'real,' stressing quality and authenticity. 'Haute Italian' describes Italian cuisine at its most elaborate, for example. Menus that change with the seasons, stressing foods fresh from local farms, are points of pride for many restaurants, as are organically grown vegetables and preservative-free meats and poultry.

Special diets

While 'vegetarian' has graduated from a regular option to a mainstay, with vegan choices increasingly available, the inclusive theme is continued with diets containing the prefix 'free' ('dairy-free' or 'gluten-free,' for example). These terms are sprinkled over menus in New York, making it possible for everyone to find suitable food, whatever their dietary requirements.

FOOD SHOPS

Vital to New York's food culture are gourmet shops, delicatessens, and bakeries. At the high end are Zabar's, Dean & Deluca, Eataly, and Barney Greengrass, which carry premium meats, fish, cheeses, baked goods, and prepared foods. More modest in size (but not quality) are mom-and-pop ethnic stores: traditional Italian and Jewish delicatessens, bagel shops, pastry shops, and Asian markets.

TRENDS BY AREA

Midtown

Some of the world's finest and most expensive restaurants – the Four Seasons, Le Bernadin, and Per Se to name but a few – are located in Midtown. Many Manhattan mainstays are here too, with the longevity prize going to the fabulous centenarian Oyster Bar at Grand Central Terminal.

For Midtown dining, it pays to do your homework. While spontaneity is fun farther downtown, in Midtown it's best to make reservations, especially to dine before or after the theater.

Restaurants here, especially the more expensive ones, often have formal dress codes. Men are suited (or at least jacketed) and women go groomed for a glamorous night on the town. Many Midtown restaurants are closed Sundays, and for lunch on Saturdays, as their corporate customers have gone.

Meatpacking District, Chelsea, Soho, and Tribeca

The Meatpacking District is good for both dining and posing, even if the patrons are often wafer-thin models who look as if they never eat. Chelsea Market, at Ninth Avenue and 15th Street, is heaven for food fetishists – a dozen or so bakeries, meat markets, kitchen suppliers, and other stores of a gastronomic bent, along with trendy dining places.

Once Soho gained recognition as an artistic center, people began streaming here in search of 'the scene.' The restaurant tariffs reflect Soho's now-dominant chicness, but there's no need to go hungry, or to pay through the nose. You can shell out $40+ for a steak at Balthazar, but you can also eat for plenty less at Fanelli Café.

Sweet treats

Street food in Lower Manhattan

In bordering Tribeca, the star element plays a big part, particularly in the shape of actor Robert De Niro. Now one of Tribeca's most famous residents, he moved here in 1976, and began investing in restaurants such as Nobu and the Tribeca Grill. He promoted his 'hood as a cool area in which to hang out, and it still is.

The bagel debate

The fastest way to start an argument among New Yorkers is to ask them where to find the best bagels in town. The rings of bread dough, first boiled then baked, were introduced to New York in the 1880s by East European Jews and have since become a local staple. They come in any number of varieties – sesame, poppy, onion, raisin, among others – and are traditionally eaten with a *schmear* of cream cheese and perhaps a slice of lox (smoked salmon) and red onion. Uptown favorites include Lenny's Bagels (2601 Broadway at 98th Street) and Tal Bagels (2446 Broadway). In Midtown, look for Ess-a-Bagel (831 Third Avenue at 50th Street) and Pick a Bagel (1101 Lexington Avenue at 61st Street). Downtown is Murray's Bagels (500 Sixth Avenue at 12th Street) and longtime favorite Kossar's (367 Grand Street near Essex Street), which specializes in 'bialys,' a close cousin to the bagel but without the hole.

East Village and Lower East Side
While once there was little reason to venture into these neighborhoods, and certainly not at night, they now come alive when the sun goes down, and, for many New Yorkers, the best two reasons to visit the Lower East Side and East Village are to drink and to dine.

The once-mean streets of the Lower East Side, an enclave of immigration in previous centuries, are now very much the domain of hipsters. To witness this renaissance, check out the restaurants around Ludlow and Clinton streets. Even the once-lowly Bowery is becoming a restaurant mecca. For a taste of the area's heritage, however, visit Katz's Delicatessen or seek out the colorful, inexpensive Indian restaurants along Sixth Street between Second and First avenues, known collectively as 'Curry Row.'

For a look at the East Village scene, check out hip bars and restaurants along avenues A and B, although expect to feel old and unfashionable if you're over 40 and out of sync if you show up before 10 o'clock.

Upper West Side
This part of town, home to the Lincoln Center and the focal point of the New York Jewish community, is good for understated neighborhood dining. Columbus Circle and the Lincoln Center area have fine-dining choices, long topped by Jean-Georges. The arrival of the Time Warner Center

In Katz's deli

upped the culinary sweepstakes (with price tags) even higher, with Michael Lomonaco's highly regarded Porter House New York, Thomas Keller's 'edible art' at Per Se (expect to pay at least $350... per person!), and the always-booked Masa, current holder of the highest price tag of any Manhattan dining experience. Keller's Bouchon Bakery offers light meals and decadent desserts with a far less stratospheric tab.

Upper East Side

With sky-high real-estate prices and stores to match, the upscale Upper East Side is where ladies of leisure like to lunch. You can dine very well indeed in this part of town, and the neighborhood demographics supply the sort of crowd that appreciates upscale dining. Many of the neighborhood's best restaurants are old standbys that seem tailor-made for special occasions, or to wine and dine a client or a visiting in-law. The neighborhood has attracted chefs such as Daniel Boulud and David Burke, in search of customers with refined taste buds and big dining budgets.

For the most part, the best restaurants are concentrated in the western part of the neighborhood, on leafy streets lined with palatial townhouses and white-glove apartment houses. In general, the farther east you go, the younger the restaurant crowd becomes – Second Avenue, especially, is noted for its noisy bars and eateries catering to restless single folk on the prowl.

BRUNCH

Weekends are when New Yorkers stroll instead of sprint. On Saturday and Sunday mornings, restaurants are filled with Manhattanites enjoying a slow start to the day, eating brunch in the company of friends, with a partner or spouse, or alone with the newspaper or a book. Sunday brunch in particular is a local tradition.

Most restaurants offer a set-price brunch menu, but there are some standout choices. In the heart of Central Park on the edge of a pond dotted with colorful rowboats, the Loeb Boathouse wins the prize for charm. The menu is good, too; try the smoked salmon frittata, French toast or steak and eggs. For the best French-inspired brunch, head for Balthazar in Soho, and dip your croissant into a gigantic cup of the house hot chocolate. For bohemian appeal, head out to Brooklyn, which excels at laidback weekends.

Food and drink prices

Throughout this book, price guide for a three-course dinner for one:

$$$$ = over $70
$$$ = $50–70
$$ = $25–50
$ = under $25

A successful shop at Macy's

SHOPPING

There are few more exciting places to shop than this Cornucopia-on-the-Hudson, with its boutiques, department stores, and discount outlets all jostling for a piece of the sales action.

From the 1860s to around 1920, shopping was concentrated in what is now the Ladies Mile Historic District. The heart was roughly from 14th to 24th streets along Sixth Avenue. But as the better residential areas continued moving north in the early 1900s, the stores followed, opening quarters in Midtown, where the larger stores remain today. Shopping, however, is not limited to any one area. Every neighborhood has its share of lures, suited to the tastes and budgets of its residents. A general rule of thumb is that the most elegant boutiques are Uptown, the big department stores are in Midtown, and the funkier boutiques are Downtown. Wherever you roam in New York, shopping is part of the fun.

Opening times vary – most department stores and many other shops open Mon–Sat from 8am or 9am to 9pm or 10pm, with shorter hours on Sundays.

Sales are held after the Christmas holidays and in mid-July. Department stores tend to offer the best markdowns. Holiday weekends – Memorial Day, Labor Day, etc. – are also prime sale times. Barney's legendary warehouse sales draw big crowds. For manufacturers' sample sales, check www.topbutton.com.

DEPARTMENT STORES

New York is still known for its department stores, selling everything from dishes to designer fashions. Macy's bills itself as 'the world's largest department store.' Bloomingdales, at 1003 Third Avenue at 60th Street (entrances also on Lexington Avenue), caters to a slightly more upscale market. A notch higher still are Saks Fifth Avenue and Bergdorf Goodman, both luxury stores selling mostly clothes and accessories. Barney's at 660 Madison Avenue and 61st Street is the *ne plus ultra* for pricey cutting-edge fashions.

WHAT TO BUY

Fashion

Look to 57th Street between 5th and Madison avenues and Madison Avenue above 60th Street for elegant, expensive boutiques, to Soho for high-end fashion, to Fifth Avenue for reliable labels, and to NoLita and the Lower East

Caps at a street market *In the Strand Book Store*

Side for cutting-edge designs and valuable vintage. The Meatpacking District is home to many high-profile designers. For high fashion at low prices, head for Century 21 Department Store (22 Cortland Street between Church Street and Broadway in Lower Manhattan), where designer labels can be had at substantial discounts. T. J. Maxx is another discount chain with several locations around town.

Art and antiques

The city has hundreds of art galleries, from major auction houses like Sotheby's to the avant-garde galleries in Chelsea. Traditional galleries tend to be found on East 57th Street and on the Upper East Side. Only a few galleries remain in Soho.

A good neighborhood for antiques is 10th and 12th streets between University Place and Broadway. Manhattan Art & Antiques Center (1050 Second Avenue at 56th Street; http://the-maac.com) has dozens of dealers under one roof. ABC Carpet & Home (888 Broadway at 19th Street; www.abchome.com) has several floors of unique furniture, accessories, and carpets from all over the world.

For flea market finds, check the weekend offerings at Hell's Kitchen Flea Market (West 39th Street between Ninth and Tenth avenues; www.annexmarkets.com), and the Green Flea Market (100 West 77th Street; www.greenfleamarkets.com).

Books

Barnes & Noble (www.barnesandnoble.com) dominates the market with its multiple superstores. They usually have cafés and weekly readings from authors both famous and soon-to-be. Greenwich Village is a great place to shop for books and records; for secondhand and antiquarian titles pay a visit to the Strand Book Store (www.strandbooks.com). They also stock a seasonal kiosk at the southeast corner of Central Park. Some unusual specialty shops include Books of Wonder for children (18 West 18th Street between Fifth and Sixth avenues; www.booksofwonder.com), Mysterious Bookshop for mysteries (58 Warren Street between West Broadway and Church Street; www.mysteriousbookshop.com), and Kitchen Arts & Letters for chefs (1435 Lexington Avenue between 93rd and 94th streets; http://kitchenartsandletters.com).

Electronics

One of the best places to buy cameras and photographic equipment is bustling B&H Photo-Video at 420 Ninth Avenue at 34th Street (tel: 212-444-6615; www.bhphotovideo.com). Opening hours vary due to Jewish holidays; call ahead.

Another good bet is Best Buy at 60 West 23rd Street. And if you want to indulge in the latest iPhone, visit the city's fabulous flagship Apple Store on Fifth Avenue.

Some smaller places don't offer warranties on electronic goods, so check before you buy.

A Jazz at Lincoln Center performance

ENTERTAINMENT

From the bright lights of Broadway to the stage of the Metropolitan Opera, symphony at Carnegie Hall to jazz or ballet at Lincoln Center, New York is America's entertainment capital, with a parade of world-class attractions.

Mention New York and most visitors think Broadway, with good reason. New York has been a theater mecca since the early 1900s, when the proliferation of bright lights earned the street the nickname of the 'Great White Way.' Around 14 million patrons attend a Broadway show in an average year.

The city has been equally important in music. The Metropolitan Opera, founded in 1880, is world-renowned, and New York has been a popular music center since the days of Tin Pan Alley in the early 1900s. The heritage continues at Lincoln Center, one of the largest performing arts centers in the world, home to eleven resident organizations including opera, ballet, symphony, chamber music, jazz, theater, and film. New York clubs, always on the cutting edge, have been influential in the development of genres from swing to jazz, rock to rap.

THEATER

Besides the dozens of theaters on and around Broadway, New York has several non-profit repertory companies, performing both new works and revivals; many of these go on to take their shows to Broadway. The city also boasts well over 100 smaller theaters with 100 to 500 seats known as 'off-Broadway,' and countless interesting venues with fewer than 100 seats known as 'off-off Broadway.' Pioneering off-Broadway companies such as Playwrights Horizons have nurtured major new works, including *Driving Miss Daisy* and Sondheim's *Sunday in the Park with George*. See listings for all shows at www.offbroadway.com.

For shows offering ticket discounts, see www.theatermania.com or www.playbill.com.

DANCE

The New York City Ballet, one of America's premier companies, has fall, spring and winter seasons in the David H. Koch Theater at Lincoln Center. Its delightful Christmas season production of *The Nutcracker* is a well-loved tradition. Another major troupe, the American Ballet Theater, visits for a spring season at the Metropolitan Opera House and a fall season at the David H. Koch Theater. New York City Center also hosts important dance groups, both modern and traditional, including Alvin Ailey and the

A trendy Hell's Kitchen bar

Martha Graham Company, and the Joyce Theater is a year-round stage for modern dance troupes from around the world.

MUSIC

At Lincoln Center, David Geffen Hall is the home stage for the New York Philharmonic while Alice Tully Hall features chamber groups. David Geffen also hosts the annual summer Mostly Mozart Festival. The Metropolitan Opera season runs from October through May, the more affordable New York City Opera performs late October through November and February through April at venues like New York City Center and BAM Howard Gilman Opera House. The Juilliard School of Music offers many free concerts by its talented faculty and students.

Jazz at Lincoln Center has expansive separate quarters at the Time Warner Center that include Dizzy's Club Coca-Cola. Other well-known jazz clubs include the Blue Note and Village Vanguard. Additionally, Harlem has legendary jazz clubs such as Minton's Playhouse. For rock and other music of the day, the Beacon Theater and the Bowery Ballroom are popular spots.

MOVIES

Film buffs will find a rich menu in New York, beginning with the Elinor Bunin Munroe Film Center and Walter Reade Theater (www.filmlinc.com), home to the Film Society of Lincoln Center and the New York Film Festival from late September through mid-October. Other theaters showing independent and art films include the Paris Theater, Cinema Village, the Angelika, the IFC Center, Film Forum, and the theater of the Museum of Modern Art. The Tribeca Film Festival begun by Robert De Niro takes place in late April.

NIGHTLIFE

The city's myriad bars and clubs offer every ambience from refined to raucous, and something for every age and taste. The late night dance club scene frequented by young New Yorkers tends to be found Downtown, in the Meatpacking District or in Hell's Kitchen, on the far west side in the 40s. Hot clubs are often hidden in unexpected places like warehouses or lofts.

Sports headliners

Sports are always in season in New York, and watching a thrilling game is fun for visitors and residents. The city offers major teams in every arena: Yankee and Mets baseball April through September, Knicks and Nets basketball October through April, Giants and Jets football September through early January, Rangers and Islanders hockey October through April, and Red Bulls soccer March through October. The US Open Tennis Championship in late August and early September is a world-class Grand Slam event. For current schedules, see www.nycgo.com (go to 'Sports').

New York saw mass-scale immigration in the 19th century

HISTORY: KEY DATES

*From a small Dutch trading post to the 'crossroads of the world,'
the rise of New York has been accompanied by civil war, mass
immigration, riots and recession, terrorism, and triumph.*

NEW AMSTERDAM

1524   Giovanni da Varrazzano is the
first European to step onto the island
known to the local Algonquin Indians
as Mannahatta.

1624   The Dutch West India Com-
pany establishes a settlement (New
Amsterdam) on the southern tip of
Mannahatta.

1664   War between England and Hol-
land. New Amsterdam surrenders and
is renamed New York after Charles II's
brother, James, Duke of York.

INDEPENDENCE TO CIVIL WAR

1776   The Revolutionary War reaches
New York; the colonies declare inde-
pendence. British troops occupy
New York until 1783.

1789–90   New York is capital of the
new United States of America.

1811   The decision is made to lay out
the city's streets in a grid pattern.

1830   Irish and German immigrants
begin arriving in great numbers.

1835   Part of Manhattan is ravaged
by the 'Great Fire.'

1848–9   Political refugees arrive after
failure of the German Revolution.

1861–5   American Civil War. The city
provides troops and supplies to the
Yankee effort. Draft riots engulf the
streets in 1863.

LATE 19TH CENTURY

1865   Italians, Jews, and Chinese
begin arriving in large numbers.

1883   The Brooklyn Bridge opens.

1886   The Statue of Liberty, a gift
from France, is unveiled.

1892   Ellis Island becomes the entry
point for immigrants. More than 12
million immigrants pass through
before it is closed in 1954.

20TH CENTURY

1902   Completion of Flatiron Building,
one of the city's tallest buildings at
the time.

1913   Erection of the world's tallest
skyscraper, the Woolworth Building,
begins. It is superseded in 1930 by
the Chrysler Building.

1917–18   US intervenes in World War I.

1929   Wall Street Crash and start of
the Great Depression.

Disaster struck with the Wall Street crash in 1929

1931 Empire State Building opens, the world's tallest building at the time.

1933–45 Europeans take refuge in New York from Nazi persecution.

1941 US enters World War II.

1946 The newly-formed United Nations chooses New York to be its permanent headquarters.

1973 The 110-story World Trade Center opens, the world's tallest building at the time.

1975 The city avoids bankruptcy via Federal government loan.

1987 'Black Monday' on Wall Street, shares drop 30 percent in value.

1993 Rudolph Giuliani voted in as mayor and gets 'tough on crime.' A bomb explodes below the World Trade Center.

21ST CENTURY

2001 Terrorists crash two hijacked planes into the Twin Towers of the World Trade Center. The buildings collapse, killing close to 3,000 people. Michael Bloomberg is elected mayor.

2003 Power blackout plunges New York into darkness. FBI survey finds New York to be the safest large city in the US.

2004 Museum of Modern Art reopens in Manhattan after major expansion.

2008 Democratic Senator Barack Obama elected the first black president of the United States. Wall Street experiences the worst financial crisis since the Great Depression.

2009 Michael Bloomberg elected for an unprecedented third term as mayor. New baseball stadiums open for the Yankees and the Mets. High Line Park opens to the public.

2011 Occupy Wall Street protesters descend on lower Manhattan.

2012 Hurricane Sandy causes extensive damage to the waterfront and transportation systems.

2013 Democrat Bill de Blasio is elected as the city's new mayor.

2014 Last section of the High Line completed.

2015 One World Trade Center, the tallest building in the Western Hemisphere (1,776ft/541 meters), opens to visitors.

2016 A homemade pressure cooker bomb explodes on a busy West 23rd Street in the Chelsea neighborhood, injuring 31 people.

2017 New York property tycoon Donald Trump is sworn in as 45th President of the United States, becoming the first New Yorker to hold office since Franklin D. Roosevelt. The Second Avenue Subway finally opens after almost a century of planning and abandoned attempts. Democrat Bill de Blasio is elected for a second term as Mayor of New York City.

2018 The NYPD reports the safest summer on record for crime in New York City. Central Park and Prospect Park becomes largely car-free, as part of a program to return the parks to their original state.

BEST ROUTES

In the Empire State Building's lobby

FIFTH AVENUE

*Few streets evoke the essence of the city as powerfully as Fifth Avenue,
with its iconic Empire State Building, glorious Rockefeller Center,
stylish shopping, and elegant St Patrick's Cathedral.*

> **DISTANCE:** 1.5 miles (2.5km)
> **TIME:** A half-day
> **START:** Empire State Building
> **END:** Grand Army Plaza
> **POINTS TO NOTE:** Try to get to
> the Empire State Building as early
> as possible to avoid long lines. Or
> come back at dusk for sunset and a
> spectacular view of Manhattan at night.
> The Top of the Rock offers an alternative
> view of the city skyline with shorter lines.

Once the playground of Gotham's
wealthiest families, today Fifth Avenue
is most people's image of Manhattan.
Here you'll find the city's most famous
skyscrapers, best views, landmark buildings, and signature stores.

EMPIRE STATE BUILDING

Rising like a rocket above 34th Street
and Fifth Avenue is the **Empire State
Building ❶** (www.esbnyc.com; observatory daily 8am–2am, last ascent at
1.15am). When it opened in 1931, this

Art Deco landmark was the tallest building in the world; today, it ranks behind
One World Trade Center and skyscrapers in Dubai, Taipei, Kuala Lumpur,
and Chicago, among others. Still, the
view from the 86th-floor Observatory is
incomparable: on a clear day you can
see as far as 80 miles (128km) away.

This is the place where a forlorn
Cary Grant waited for Deborah Kerr in
An Affair to Remember (1957), where
Tom Hanks hooked up with Meg Ryan in
Sleepless in Seattle (1993), and where
Fay Wray had a rendezvous with a tall,
dark leading man of a more brutish dis-
position in *King Kong* (1933).

Ticket options

Lines at the security checkpoint, ticket
booth, and elevator can be horrendous,
but you can save time by buying tickets
online. Although you still have to pass
through security and wait for an elevator, you won't need to wait hours to get
a ticket. If you have money to burn, you
could buy a 'VIP Express Pass,' entitling
the holder to move to the front of all lines.
For an additional fee, you can also pur-

At the Rockefeller Center

Surveying the Empire State Building

chase tickets which allow access to both the 86th-floor and 102nd-floor **Observatory**. Comprehensive NY CityPASS and NYC It All Tour are also good value alternatives if you plan to visit other attractions.

NEW YORK PUBLIC LIBRARY

Continue north on legendary Fifth Avenue. Although the magnificent townhouses once owned here by such eminent dynasties as the Astors and Vanderbilts have been replaced by less glamorous discount shops, the old grandeur can still be found at the elegant Beaux Arts **New York Public Library** ❷ (www.nypl.org; Mon and Thu–Sat 10am–6pm, Tue–Wed until 8pm; Sun 1–5pm; free access and tours at 11am & 2pm Mon–Sat; 2pm Sun) at 42nd Street, renamed the Stephen A. Schwarzman Building after a large donation from the billionaire investor.

With its Corinthian columns and white Vermont marble, its palatial staircases, and famous sculpted lions standing guard out front, the 1911 building is a landmark of its kind. The building's architects were John Merven Carrère and Thomas Hastings, Paris-trained partners who triumphed in a design competition. The grand stone lions at the entrance were sculpted by Edward Clark Potter and are known as Patience and Fortitude, nicknames bestowed upon them by Depression-era Mayor Fiorello LaGuardia.

Reading Room

Not to be missed is the majestic third-floor Rose Main Reading Room, brilliantly renovated in 2016 at a cost of $12 million. Its vast perimeter is lined with reference works surrounding lamp-lit desks, at which readers digest books summoned with 'call slips' from the library's vast hidden recesses. Free tours are offered daily from Astor Hall at the library's entrance.

Among the books, maps, manuscripts, periodicals, photographs, and varied items numbering in the millions in this building are the first Guten-

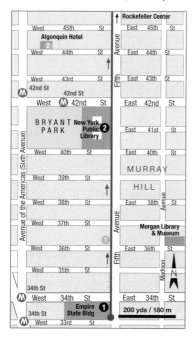

The New York Public Library's Reading Room

The Morgan Library & Museum

Billionaire J.P. Morgan (1837–1913), known for his consolidation of railroad and steel empires, was an expert collector with taste and wealth, both well displayed at the Morgan Library & Museum (225 Madison Avenue at 36th Street; www.themorgan.org; Tue–Thu 10.30am–5pm, Fri 10.30am–9pm, Sat 10am–6pm, Sun 11am–6pm). Around the turn of the 20th century, Morgan acquired entire collections from the most prominent art dealers in Europe and the United States. He bought Chinese ceramics, medieval tapestries, and Near Eastern antiquities along with Old Master paintings and drawings. He also acquired illuminated books of hours, and handwritten letters by Thomas Jefferson, George Washington, and Napoleon, as well as manuscripts by Charles Dickens, John Keats, John Milton, and others. Equally impressive is the building, an elegant mansion with a fabulous library for Morgan, designed in the early 1900s by architect Charles McKim. The modern extension by Renzo Piano substantially increased the library's exhibition space, and added two excellent lunch options, a café, and a formal dining room. A nearby alternative for lunch is the gourmet Franco-Italian **Ai Fiori** in The Langham, see ❶.

berg Bible brought to America, Christopher Columbus's 1493 account of his momentous voyage, George Washington's own handwritten *Farewell Address*, and Thomas Jefferson's early draft of the *Declaration of Independence*.

Head two blocks north to West 44th Street for a liquid lunch at the **Algonquin Hotel**, see ❷.

ROCKEFELLER CENTER

Continuing up Fifth Avenue, a left turn at West 47th Street leads into the **Diamond District** ❸, where close to $500 million in gems is traded every day, much of it by Hasidic Jews.

At 48th Street, you will find the glorious **Rockefeller Center** ❹ (tours daily every hour; tickets sold at the NBC Experience Store or at www.rockefellercenter.com), a complex of 19 commercial buildings that were constructed by the financier John D. Rockefeller, Jr, in the 1930s.

Enter this vast 'city within a city' from Fifth via the **Channel Gardens**, a sloping walkway that leads to the base of the **Comcast Building** (30 Rockefeller Plaza; also known as 30 Rock), a soaring 1933 Art Deco landmark that in some ways presaged the skyscrapers to come.

Public art

The Comcast Building is fronted by a sunken courtyard that becomes the venue of an outdoor restaurant during the summer and an ice-skating rink

City views from the Top of the Rock

in winter. A towering Christmas tree stands here in the holiday season.

Lee Lawrie's stone-relief *Genius* looms over the building's entrance, while inside the main lobby are two murals by José María Sert, *American Progress* and *Time*. Mexican muralist Diego Rivera was originally to do the murals, but the Rockefellers fired him for refusing to change a panel that depicted Bolshevik revolution-

ary and Soviet leader Vladimir Lenin. The unfinished mural was shrouded in canvas during the building's opening ceremony and, six months later, destroyed.

Television tour

Before leaving, take a look in the **NBC Experience Store** (entrance on 49th Street; www.thetouratnbcstudios.com; tours Mon–Thu 8.20am–2.20pm, Fri until 5pm, Sat–Sun until 6pm), across from the glassed-in Today Show studio. There are quirky interactive exhibits and a collection of memorabilia from the network's 80-year history. However, the highlight is the 70-minute behind-the-scenes **NBC Studio Tour**.

Top of the Rock

Also available are tickets for the **Top of the Rock** (www.topoftherocknyc.com; daily 8am–midnight, last ascent 11pm), an observation deck on the 70th floor of the Comcast Building. If you don't have time for the Empire State, this is a good alternative, as the lines tend to be shorter, the observation deck less crowded, and the views include Central Park. The observation deck is also glassed in, rather than protected by railings, so views here are less interrupted. The **Rock Center Café**, see ③, is a good refueling option.

ST PATRICK'S CATHEDRAL

Back on street level, a huge bronze sculpture of *Atlas*, also by Lee Lawrie, stands in front of the **International Building**,

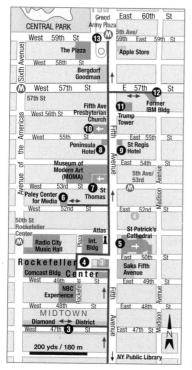

St Patrick's Cathedral

between 50th and 51st streets. **St Patrick's Cathedral** ❺ (http://saintpatrickscathedral.org; daily 6.30am–8.45pm), on the other side of Fifth Avenue, towers over the scene. Dedicated in 1879, St Patrick's ornate neo-Gothic facade works as an intriguing counterpoint to the angular lines and smooth surfaces of the surrounding skyscrapers. Take time to admire the cathedral's interior, notably its impressive stained glass.

Just north of the Cathedral on Fifth Avenue is **Fig & Olive** ❹, another pleasant spot for lunch.

THE PALEY CENTER FOR MEDIA

For a restful nostalgia stop, detour west half a block on 52nd Street to the **Paley Center for Media** ❻ (25 East 52nd Street; http://media.paleycenter.org; Wed–Sun noon–6pm, Thu until 8pm). Named for William Paley, former head of the CBS network, this is a rare treasure trove of 150,000 radio and television programs from their earliest days. In the fourth-floor library, you can sit at a screen and have your choice of hundreds of vintage shows, from *I Love Lucy* to *The Honeymooners*. Helpful staff will show you how to navigate. The downstairs auditorium shows films with themes such as 'Funny Women of TV.'

SHOPPING STOPS

From here Fifth Avenue is mostly devoted to commerce, although several churches do counterbalance the materialism to a degree. **Saks Fifth Avenue**, one of the country's best department stores, is across from Rockefeller Center. The super-rich can be seen gliding between Versace, Cartier, Gucci, and other shops from 51st to 57th streets. Don't forget to pay tribute to one of the most famous scenes in American cinema history and look in the windows at **Tiffany's**, in homage to Audrey Hepburn as Holly Golightly.

53RD TO 56TH STREETS

The ornate facade of **St Thomas Church** ❼ – built in French Gothic style and completed in 1913 – overlooks Fifth Avenue from 53rd Street. If time allows, stop to admire the sanctuary.

Continue to the end of the next block. On the left is the **Peninsula Hotel** ❽, housed in a grand 1905 Renaissance building, which caters mostly to the corporate elite. On the right, the even grander **St Regis Hotel** ❾ (see page 107) is an Edwardian wedding cake of a building, adorned with marvelous filigree and murals by Maxfield Parrish.

Across West 55th Street from the Peninsula Hotel is the stately **Fifth Avenue Presbyterian Church** ❿, built in Gothic style in 1873.

Rising from the corner of 56th Street is **Trump Tower** ⓫. Step into the lobby of this 68-story condominium complex for a glimpse of tycoon-turned-president Donald Trump's signature over-

Cabs on Fifth Avenue

The Plaza at night

the-top style, replete with gleaming brass, polished marble, and a five-story waterfall.

57TH STREET

There's shopping galore around the corner on East 57th Street, home to designers including Louis Vuitton, Chanel, and Dior. Also nearby are stores for more casual brands such as UGG and Coach.

Need a break? Wander into the glass-enclosed atrium of the former **IBM Building** ⑫ (590 Madison Avenue), where footsore shoppers can have a rest surrounded by modern sculpture, or enjoy a snack on the mezzanine.

GRAND ARMY PLAZA

Beyond 57th Street, it's a one-block walk past upscale department store **Bergdorf Goodman** (women's fashions are in the main store on the west side of Fifth, men's on the east; www.bergdorfgoodman.com) to **Grand Army Plaza** ⑬, which serves as a gateway to Central Park and the setting of the city's landmark grande dame hotel, **The Plaza** (see page 107). It is now home to apartment dwellers too, but the classic style remains.

Food and drink

① AI FIORI
400 Fifth Avenue (The Langham, 2nd level); tel: 212-613-8660; daily B, Br, L and D; $$
Michelin-starred French-Italian cuisine is the order of the day at this stylish spot in The Langham apartment building, with superb breakfast and brunch also on offer.

② ALGONQUIN HOTEL
59 West 44th Street (near Sixth Avenue); tel: 212-840-6800; www.algonquinhotel.com; daily B, L, and D; $$$
Whether it's Martinis at the Blue Bar or afternoon tea in the woodpaneled lobby, there's a sense of literary history in the space once occupied by Dorothy Parker and other members of the Round Table.

③ ROCK CENTER CAFÉ
20 West 50th Street; tel: 212-332-7620; www.rockcentercafeny.com; daily B, Br, L, and D; $$
Winter views of the ice-skating rink make this a cheery place to enjoy Italian fare (the crab and risotto cakes are a standout) and hearty American breakfasts. In summer the rink is converted to garden setting.

④ FIG & OLIVE
10 East 52nd Street (between Fifth and Madison avenues); tel: 212-319-2002; www.figandolive.com; Mon–Sun L, Sat–Sun also Br, daily D; $$$
Interesting Mediterranean menu featuring paellas, pasta dishes, risottos, and more. Brunch is a more international affair, with avocado toast, steak and eggs, and French omelet among other favorites.

In busy Times Square

TIMES SQUARE TO HERALD SQUARE

Spend a few hours around Times Square and Broadway, exploring one of the world's largest stores and two unique museums, and purchase discount tickets if you want to end the day with a Broadway show.

DISTANCE: 2 miles (3km)
TIME: A half-day
START: Times Square at the corner of 42nd street
END: Herald Square, Sixth Avenue and 34th–35th streets
POINTS TO NOTE: Our suggestion is to do some sightseeing, followed by a Broadway show. On Wednesdays and weekends you could end a morning tour with lunch and a matinee, otherwise start in the afternoon to finish with an evening show.

TIMES SQUARE

New York's 'Crossroads of the World,' **Times Square ❶**, spanning from 42nd to 46th streets on Broadway (the only street north of 14th that doesn't fit the grid format), swirls with irrepressible energy from the masses of people and the eye-popping neon wattage. Yet it is safer and more family-friendly than ever, since much of Broadway is now car-free.

42ND STREET

The biggest transformation is once-seedy 42nd Street, now home to Disney theaters, movie complexes, clubs, and the always-popular **Madame Tussaud's Wax Museum ❷** (www.madametussauds.com/newyork; hours vary widely throughout the year, but generally Sun–Thu 10am–8pm, Fri–Sat 10am–10pm; order online for savings of up to $5), filled with happy visitors taking snaps with the amazingly lifelike wax figures of celebrities from Brad Pitt to Abraham Lincoln.

Theater district

This area has been the heart of Manhattan's theater district for over a century, with great heritage and history to soak up. Walk west half a block on 44th Street for **Shubert Alley ❸** and the 1912 Shubert Theater (www.shubert.nyc), headquarters for the once-famous impresario. Hopeful actors used to line up here hoping to be cast in a show. Detour half a block east at 45th Street to see the 1902

The city never sleeps

Lyceum Theatre ❹ (149 West 45th Street), the oldest continually operating theater, with an elegant columned Beaux Arts facade and mansard roof.

This is also the heart of media land, so look out on Broadway around 44th Street for the second-story **ABC Studio** ❺, 1500 Broadway, from which *Good Morning America* is broadcast on weekday mornings, and the **MTV Studio** ❻, where it's not unusual to see squealing teens on the sidewalk, hoping for a glimpse of their American idols.

For a pitstop, there are two good options on 44th Street. **Café Un Deux Trois** ❶, a busy brasserie, is between Sixth and Seventh avenues, while **Carmine's** ❷, a longtime family-style Italian favorite, is further west, past Broadway.

For available discount tickets, visit the **TKTS** booth ❼ at Duffy Square on 46th Street. The tiered red-glass staircase at the rear is a fine perch for taking in the sea of neon.

You'll see other legendary theaters as you continue up Broadway. The **Palace Theatre**, near 47th Street, was a vaudeville mainstay featuring stars like George Jessel, Bob Hope, and Will Rogers; opened in 1913, it was closed at the time of writing for extensive renovations. The 1925 Hammerstein's Theater between 53rd and 54th, renamed the **Ed Sullivan Theater**, presently hosts *The Late Show with Stephen Colbert*.

SIXTH AVENUE

The second half of this walk is a change of pace, with enticing architecture, as well as museum and shop-

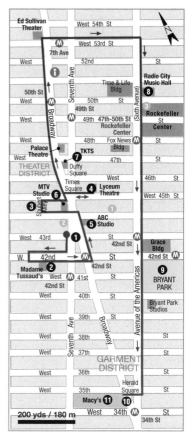

Radio City Music Hall

ping stops. Turn right at Broadway and 53rd Street and continue to Sixth Avenue and head Downtown. You are walking through a canyon of high-rise glass office buildings, a quintessential New York streetscape. Note that many of the skyscrapers, such as the Time-Life Building on 50th Street, have plazas with seating to rest weary feet and watch the busy business world go by. If you are feeling hungry at this point, as well as weary, head to **Au Bon Pain**, see ③. Located on Rockefeller Plaza, it is a handy place to stop for a sandwich.

On the west corner of 50th Street is **Radio City Music Hall** ❽, the city's grandest theater space. Built in 1932 as a palace for the people, both the exterior and interior are magnificent and the acoustics are excellent. From the massive chandeliers in the Grand Lobby to the plush, scalloped auditorium, Radio City is the last word in Art Deco extravagance. The Stuart Davis mural that once graced the men's smoking lounge is now owned by the Museum of Modern Art. Join a tour (www.radiocity.com; daily 9.30am–5pm) or take in a show to see for yourself.

Continuing on Sixth Avenue, you'll know the Fox Network headquarters at 48th Street by the illuminated latest news headlines across the building, and will pass the 'Little Brazil' area, so named for its many South American restaurants, at 46th Street.

Via Brasil (see page 114) is a great place to sample the cuisine.

BRYANT PARK

Bryant Park ❾ (www.bryantpark. org) is a green garden oasis located behind the Public Library from 42nd Street to 40th Street. Stop here for coffee and a snack.

Bryant Park is the scene of much activity: a carousel, an outdoor reading room stocked with books and magazines, and chess tables. The park also hosts outdoor movies in summer and the city's only free ice skating in winter (skate rental costs $20).

LANDMARK ARCHITECTURE

Across from Bryant Park on 40th Street are two landmark New York buildings worth a short detour. Look up above the ground-floor shops to appreciate **Bryant Park Studios**, 80 West 40th at the corner of Sixth Avenue. It was built in 1901 in Beaux Arts style by an artist who insisted on huge windows to capture natural light.

Such notables as the photographer Edward Steichen and the painter Fernand Léger once had studios in the building, which is currently occupied by many design firms.

The former American Standard Building at 40 West 40th Street, an early design by Raymond Hood of

Sunny Bryant Park

Herald Square

Rockefeller Center fame, was built in 1923–4 of dark brick topped with gold, so that when illuminated at night the building resembles a glowing radiator coil. It was recently converted into the **Bryant Park Hotel** (http://bryantparkhotel.com), but the elaborate landmark facade could not be altered.

HERALD SQUARE

Now make your way to 35th Street and a chance to relax and regroup in **Herald Square** ❿, converted into a small green city park with seating under shady umbrellas, a kiosk selling refreshments and that rare amenity, a well-maintained public bathroom. It is the perfect place to relax before heading across the street to one of the world's largest stores.

MACY'S

Founded in 1858 on 34th Street, **Macy's** ⓫ moved to this location in 1902, when it installed the first escalators seen in a department store. You can still see some of the original wooden escalators today. Nine shopping floors and a cellar store stretching for a square block will surely hold something to tempt shoppers.

If you prefer a Broadway show to shopping, Times Square is just one stop away, Uptown on the N or R subway train from 34th Street.

Food and drink

① CAFÉ UN DEUX TROIS
123 West 44th Street (between Broadway and Sixth Avenue); tel: 212-354-4148; www.cafeundeuxtrois.com; daily B, L, and D; $$
This large, hectic pre-theater favorite is a good choice for reliable, if not spectacular, brasserie fare, notably decent *pommes frites*. Crayons and butcher paper keep fidgety kids occupied.

② CARMINE'S
200 West 44th Street (between Seventh and Eighth avenues); tel: 212-221-3800; www.carminesnyc.com; daily L and D; $$$
This theater land institution piles plates high with hearty Southern Italian fare, from home-style lasagna and bolognese to broiled lobster and baked clams.

③ AU BON PAIN
30 Rockefeller Plaza (50th Street between Fifth and Sixth avenues); tel: 212-757-4628; www.aubonpain.com; daily B, L, and D; $
When all you want is a good, inexpensive sandwich, this chain delivers, with orders all freshly made. You'll spot other locations all over town.

MoMa's gift store

MUSEUM OF MODERN ART

The world's premier modern art museum is home to a fabulous collection of Picassos, Warhols, and Pollocks, as well as groundbreaking Architecture and Design exhibits. The building alone is worth a visit.

DISTANCE: N/A – the whole tour is spent in the museum
TIME: A half-day
START/END: MoMA
POINTS OF NOTE: The museum is free to enter on Fridays from 4–8 pm. Audio players can be borrowed free of charge from a desk in the lobby.

The **Museum of Modern Art** ❶ (MoMA; 11 West 53rd Street, between Fifth and Sixth avenues; daily 10.30am–5.30pm, Fri until 8pm; free Fri 4–8pm) was a daring pioneer when it opened in 1928 and has been hugely influential in the development of modern art.

A dazzling expansion, completed in 2004, almost doubled the size of the Museum of Modern Art and was the first project for architect Yoshio Taniguchi outside his native Japan. His design has provided soaring spaces for oversize sculptures, and natural light from wide windows and a 110ft (33.5-meter) sky-lit central atrium extending from the second to sixth floors. The stairwells and pathways with picture windows display art as well as providing views of the sculpture garden and of people moving between galleries through corridors across the garden.

Adjacent to the main MoMA building is 53W53 (53 West 53rd Street), an impressive glass skyscraper slated for opening in 2019. It will house extra gallery space for the museum as well as luxurious apartments.

THE COLLECTION

At the heart of MoMA's collection are around 3,600 paintings and sculptures dating from the 1880s, a time that heralded the beginnings of the modern sensibility and a move away from conventional figurative representation.

In addition to these, MoMA's holdings include countless drawings and prints, books, important photo and film collections, and a notable range of functional objects that exhibit good design: from chairs to cups and saucers.

Museum layout

Some visitors will want to head directly

The building is designed to let in lots of light

to the fifth floor, where the sequence of galleries dedicated to the core collection of painting and sculpture begins; it continues on the fourth floor. You will notice that this is not the sort of museum to arrange art into neat categories. Instead, the galleries flow into one another with a minimum of signage and interpretation, reflecting the museum's view that there is 'no one history of modern art.' Their entire collection isn't always on display. If you want to know if you will see a particular work during your visit, use the search function at www.moma.org.

MoMA's third floor deals with photography, architecture and design, and drawings. The second floor contains the contemporary galleries, sections devoted to prints and illustrated books, and a café. On the first floor is a more formal restaurant, the museum's store, and the sculpture garden.

FIFTH FLOOR

In Gallery 1, there are many famous Post-Impressionist works. Among them are Paul Cézanne's *Milk Can with Apples* (1879–80) and *Self-Portrait in a Straw Hat* (1875–6) and Vincent van Gogh's *The Starry Night* (1889) and *The Olive Trees (1889).*

The range of styles grouped together as Post-Impressionists is startling. Contrast Georges Seurat's studies in optical effects epitomized in the seascape *Port-en-Bessin, Entrance to the Harbor* (1888) with Paul Gauguin's works showing influ-

ences of African and Polynesian culture, such as *Washerwomen* (1888) and *The Seed of the Areoi* (1892). Meanwhile, Henri Rousseau's mix of fantasy and naivety is reflected in *The Sleeping Gypsy* (1897) and *The Dream* (1910).

Pablo Picasso, Henri Matisse, and Claude Monet

The next few galleries take the visitor through the transition to Modernism. The central protagonist artistically was Pablo Picasso. If it is on display, compare *Boy Leading a Horse* (1906) with *Les Demoiselles d'Avignon* (1907), which announced the arrival of Cubism. Picasso's great rival, Matisse, is also well represented. In his dreamlike *The Red Studio* (1911), the artist experiments with color and space and depicts his Paris studio as a flat red rectangle with his works on the walls.

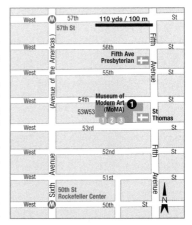

Admiring art

Gallery 9 is set aside for Monet's luminous *Water Lilies*, rendered late in life at his garden in Giverny, France.

Beyond Realism

Other fifth-floor galleries chart the paths of more great names in nonfigurative early 20th-century art. Here are the Cubist explorations of Georges Braque and Fernand Léger, and the abstract works of Dutch-born Piet Mondrian.

In Gallery 12, the Surrealists make good their escape from physical representation into the psychic world of dreams and the subconscious. Famous Surrealist works include Joan Miró's *The Birth of the World* (1925), Salvador Dalí's *The Persistence of Memory* (1931), with its melting clocks, and René Magritte's *The False Mirror* (1928).

Edward Hopper and Andrew Wyeth

Not that all artists abandoned Realism. Edward Hopper's brooding *House by the Railroad* (1925), which epitomizes the artist's sense of isolation, was the first painting acquired by the museum. Realism also was similarly embraced by the idiosyncratic Andrew Wyeth, whose *Christina's World* (1948) is one of MoMA's most popular works.

FOURTH FLOOR

The trail resumes in Gallery 15 on the fourth floor, where works by Adolph Gottlieb, Arshile Gorky and Lee Krasner (who was married to fellow artist Jack-son Pollock) embody individual brands of abstraction.

Abstract Expressionism

Spaces devoted to members of the so-called 'New York School' start in galleries 16 and 17 with works by Pollock, whose 'action paintings' were created by dripping paint onto large canvases laid flat on the floor. Equally arresting is Willem de Kooning's *Woman, I* (1950–2).

While these artists were developing a visual language of movement and verve, 'Color Field' painters such as Mark Rothko preferred to work with broad, even expanses of deep color, as in *No. 16 (Red, Brown, and Black) (1958)*.

Robert Rauschenberg and Jasper Johns

Farther along are works by artists who depicted a world brimming with the detritus of consumer culture. Robert Rauschenberg's signature style was objects splattered with paint – such as his *Bed* (1955). Also found here is one of Jasper John's 'recontextualized' icons: the potent symbol of the American flag.

Pop Art

Andy Warhol's *Gold Marilyn Monroe* (1962) draws visitors into a large gallery (No. 23) devoted to the pop artists of the 1960s and '70s. The theme of Pop Art was consumer culture and the mass media. Warhol's *Campbell's Soup Cans* (1962) and images of celebrities highlight the commodification of

'War in Vietnam'   *Picasso's 'Woman Dressing Her Hair'*

images. Often working with silkscreen prints, which he produced serially, Warhol sought not only to make art out of mass-produced items but to mass-produce the art itself. Roy Lichtenstein's comic-book paintings are represented here by *Bauhaus Stairway* (1988).

THIRD FLOOR

The design department on this floor highlights the aesthetics of functional design. There is furniture by designers including Charles Eames, Le Corbusier, and Frank Lloyd Wright, and 'everyday' items such as vacuum cleaners, kettles, computers, and a Bell & Howell helicopter. Some of the more everyday products on show in the design department on the third floor are still being produced today, and can be purchased in the museum's whizzy, whimsical store on the opposite (south) side of West 53rd Street.

The third floor also has sections on photography, architecture, and drawing. The photography department is particularly strong, as MoMA began collecting in the 1930s, well before most other major museums.

SECOND FLOOR

This floor holds the contemporary galleries (1980–present), displaying the latest advances in painting, sculpture, and installation. Also here are sections devoted to illustrated books and prints.

REFRESHMENT STOPS

When you are in need of refreshment, consider visiting one of the museum cafés, **Terrace 5** ❶ or **Café 2** ❷, or the more formal **The Modern** ❸. Afterwards, you may decide to stroll around the sculpture garden which was designed by Philip Johnson in 1953.

Food and drink

❶ **TERRACE 5**
MoMA, Fifth Floor; Sat–Thu 11am–5pm, Fri until 7.30pm; $
This stylish café overlooking the sculpture garden is a good choice for ice cream, tarts, and a variety of light, savory dishes. Open to museum visitors only.

❷ **CAFÉ 2**
MoMA, Second Floor; Sat–Thu 11am–5pm, Fri until 7.30pm; $
This modern interpretation of the museum cafeteria sits guests at long wooden tables to enjoy panini, antipasti, and pasta. Visitors only.

❸ **THE MODERN**
MoMA, First Floor; tel: 212-333-1220; www.themodernnyc.com; Mon–Fri L and D, Sat D; the Bar Room Mon–Sat 11.30am–10.30pm, Sun until 9.30pm; $$$$
This dining room serves gourmet contemporary cuisine. In the Bar Room you can enjoy drinks in less formal surroundings.

UNITED NATIONS AND MIDTOWN EAST

A tour of the UN followed by a visit to several Midtown landmarks, including Grand Central Terminal, the Chrysler Building, the Waldorf Astoria Hotel, and the Citigroup Center.

DISTANCE: 2 miles (3km)
TIME: A half- to full day
START: UN Building
END: 550 Madison Avenue
POINTS TO NOTE: The closest station to the UN is Grand Central/42nd Street, four blocks west.

This tour covers the central part of Manhattan east of Fifth Avenue, focusing on 42nd Street, Madison Avenue, and Park Avenue, which are home to some of New York's finest architectural landmarks.

UN HEADQUARTERS

Start at the **United Nations (UN) Headquarters** ❶ (First Avenue between 42nd and 48th streets; http://visit.un.org; year-round Mon–Fri 9am–4.45pm; guided tours currently depart from the Visitor's Center at 3.45pm daily, or a different time by request), which is situated on an 18-acre (7-hectare) campus pur-

chased by tycoon John D. Rockefeller, Jr, and donated in 1946. Technically, this is international territory, with its own firefighters, police force, and postal service.

Architecture

Designed by a committee of architects led by Wallace K. Harrison and inspired by French architect Le Corbusier, the complex is dominated by the sleek glass slab of the Secretariat building. It is, in turn, dwarfed by the neighboring 72-story **Trump World Tower**, owned by Donald Trump.

Guided tours

The only way to see the building is by guided tour, but reservations are only necessary for groups of 40 or more people. All tours start in the General Assembly building, entrance at 46th Street and 1st Avenue, and last around 45 minutes–1 hour. They usually include a visit to the Security Council Chamber, the Trusteeship Council, and General Assembly Hall. Occasionally, visitors are also allowed to watch the proceedings

The United Nations building and New York skyline from the East River

of the General Assembly or other committees. (Ask at the information desk about this.)

Artworks and artifacts donated by member countries are exhibited across the complex. These include murals by Fernand Léger, a stained-glass window by Marc Chagall, and ancient Indian and Egyptian artifacts.

Japan Society

A short walk a block and a half northwest from the UN on 47th Street and a worthwhile detour is the **Japan Society** (333 East 47th Street; www.japan-society.org: Tue–Thu noon–7pm, Fri until 9pm, Sat–Sun 11am–5pm during exhibitions), dedicated to fostering understanding and cultural exchange between Japan and the US. Changing exhibits of Japanese arts are set against a stunning backdrop of indoor gardens, a reflecting pool, and a waterfall. Opened in 1971, the building designed by Junzo Yoshimura was the first in New York by a leading Japanese architect.

EAST 42ND STREET

Head back to the corner of 42nd Street and First Avenue, where a steep stairway festooned with banners leads to **Tudor City ❷**. This classic apartment complex dates from the 1920s, when land along the East River was used for slums and slaughterhouses; hence the windows face west toward the Hudson River.

Ford Foundation Building

At this point you can either climb the stairs or loop around the block, with both options leading to the **Ford Foundation Building ❸**, near the corner of 42nd Street and Second Avenue. Behind its sheer gray walls is a 12-story atrium thick with vegetation; constructed in 1967, the Ford was one of the first

Grand Central in the holiday season

Race to the top

When auto magnate Walter Chrysler learned in 1929 that the proposed Bank of Manhattan on Wall Street would be taller than his own unfinished eponymous skyscraper, he was determined not to be undone in his ambition to construct the world's tallest building and demanded his architect, William Van Alen, add height to the Chrysler Building's spire. Van Alen's rival was his estranged business partner Craig Severance, who, on learning of Van Alen's brief, raised the height of his own tower; he declared the 925ft (282-meter) Wall Street building to be a world record-breaker in November 1929.

What Severance didn't know was that Van Alen was constructing a 180ft (60-meter) spire within the Chrysler Building. Shortly after Severance's announcement, workmen hoisted the spire into place, pushing the Chrysler's Building's height to 1,046ft (319 meters).

However, only a few months later, in April 1930, the Empire State Building was unveiled, with the addition of a mooring mast for airships that meant it surpassed the Chrysler Building by more than 200ft (60 meters). When the World Trade Center's Twin Towers were destroyed on September 11, 2001, the Empire State again became the city's tallest structure, only to be unseated again by One World Trade Center in 2014.

US buildings to utilize urban space in this pioneering way.

Superman

Walk west on 42nd Street to the **News Building** ❹ (220 East 42nd Street), an Art Deco skyscraper completed in 1930 and, until the mid-1990s, home to the *Daily News*, for years the nation's largest-circulation daily newspaper. When location scouts were looking for a setting to double as the office of the *Daily Planet*, the fictional paper for which Clark Kent and Lois Lane write in the *Superman* movies, this was the building they chose. Design highlights include the giant revolving globe.

Cambodian lunch

For lunch to-go, sneak south one block and visit **Num Pang** ❶ at 41st and Lexington, where Cambodian cooking is delivered fast and fresh in the form of sandwiches, salads and soups.

CHRYSLER BUILDING

Return to 42nd Street and the **Chrysler Building** ❺ (405 Lexington Avenue). Commissioned by auto czar Walter Chrysler, the skyscraper, considered by many to be the most beautiful in New York – if not the world – and the enduring symbol of the glamorous Art Deco era, features automotive motifs such as gargoyles inspired by radiator caps. For a few months in 1930,

Grand Central Station

The station's iconic clock

it was the tallest building in the world (see box). Inside, the marble lobby, the ceiling mural by Edward Trumbull, and lavishly decorated elevator doors are in stylistic harmony with the Art Deco exterior of the building.

GRAND CENTRAL TERMINAL

Continue on 42nd Street past the Grand Hyatt Hotel to the Beaux Arts-style **Grand Central Terminal** ❻, designed by the architecture firms of Reed & Stern and Warren & Wetmore, which opened in 1913 after 10 years of construction. The Municipal Art Society (www.mas.org) offers guided tours (daily 12.30pm) of Grand Central Terminal. Buy tickets and meet at the information booth on the main concourse.

Main concourse
Enter the terminal and follow signs to the main concourse, a cavernous barrel-vaulted chamber with enormous arched windows. Note the turquoise ceiling, painted with 2,500 stars by French artist Paul Helleu; oddly, the sky was painted back to front. At the concourse's center is the rendezvous point: the information booth, crowned by an iconic clock with four faces made of opal.

At the eastern end of the main concourse is **Grand Central Market**, which shelters numerous gourmet bakers, cheesemongers, and other purveyors of specialty foods.

Lower level and balcony
If you are hungry, there are several options. Head to the vaulted lower level for the **Oyster Bar** ❷, one of the classic New York dining experiences, or **Cipriani Dolci** ❸, which overlooks the main concourse. The lower-level Grand Central Dining Concourse offers a potpourri of stalls serving American and ethnic foods at reasonable prices. For cocktails in a stylish Italianate setting, try the **Campbell** ❹.

MADISON AVENUE

When you are finished in Grand Central, go back to 42nd Street and turn right onto **Madison Avenue**: at this point archetypal New York, with a skyline bristling with gleaming glass towers and streets typically jammed with taxis.

Villard Houses
At Madison and 50th Street, behind St Patrick's Cathedral (see page 31), are the **Villard Houses** ❼, built in 1884 by architects McKim, Mead, and White in the style of an Italian Renaissance palace. The mansions were originally intended for journalist and railway tycoon Henry Villard, who suffered bankruptcy before construction was completed, and were later occupied by the Archdiocese of New York.

In the late 1970s, two of the Villard mansions were incorporated into the **Lotte New York Palace**, where you

Madison Avenue

can now enjoy afternoon tea under a lovely vaulted ceiling created by McKim, Mead, and White.

PARK AVENUE

About a block and a half to the east, at **Park Avenue** between 49th and 50th streets, is another New York landmark, the Art Deco **Waldorf Astoria Hotel** ❽ (301 Park Avenue). At the time of writing, the Waldorf Astoria was closed for extensive renovations, although marveling at the exterior is still a must. On re-opening it promises to be even more impressive than ever on the inside; it's planned for 2021, but don't be surprised if there are further delays.

As you leave the Waldorf, look south down Park Avenue for a view of the floridly ornamented **Helmsley Building**, recognizable by its gold-and-green spire. Looming behind it is the **MetLife Building**, designed partly by Bauhaus founder Walter Gropius. With its absence of detailing and heavy lines, this 1963 behemoth became one of the most despised buildings in the city when it went up, blocking the vistas up and down Park Avenue.

A block north of the Waldorf, between 50th and 51st streets, is **St Bartholomew's Episcopal Church** ❾, a domed Byzantine-style structure consecrated in 1918. The low-level building injects a welcome sense of proportion to the skyscrapers towering around it.

Continue a block north on Park Avenue toward the 1958 **Seagram Building** ❿, designed by Mies Van der Rohe and Philip Johnson and an early example of curtain-wall construction (in which the facade of a building does not support any load other than its own).

The Citigroup Center

Turn right at 53rd Street and walk another block to the **Citigroup Center** ⓫, at 601 Lexington Avenue. Completed in 1978, the building's angled roof, which was originally designed to hold solar panels, is now a distinctive feature of the Manhattan skyline. The whole aluminum-clad, 59-story structure is propped up on pillars in order to leave room below for the equally modern-looking **St Peter's Lutheran Church**, known for its upbeat 'jazz vespers' service on Sundays at 6pm. The Citigroup's atrium market houses a number of stores and restaurants.

550 Madison Avenue

As you exit Citigroup Center, pause to look at the distinctive oval **Lipstick Building** ⓬ (885 Third Avenue at 54th Street). The lobby is open to the public. If you're craving pub grub in a legendary saloon, pop in for a pint and burger at **P.J. Clarke's** ❺ on the corner of 55th Street and Third Avenue.

At 55th Street, turn right, and return to Madison Avenue, where **No. 550** ⓭ (formerly the Sony Building), designed

The Chippendale top of 550 Madison Avenue

by Philip Johnson, rises 37 stories to a so-called 'Chippendale' top, i.e. in the shape of a broken pediment, as in the style of the English cabinetmaker's storage furniture.

Consider ending the tour by turning left off Madison Avenue to East 56th Street for a glimpse of **Trump Tower**, the ultimate emblem of Donald Trump's real estate empire. You may be content to gawp at the black crystalline exterior, or prefer to pass security into the gilded lobby, which can safely be described as 'gaudy.'

Food and drink

① NUM PANG
140 East 41st Street (between Third and Lexington avenues); tel: 212-867-8889; www.numpangkitchen.com; Mon–Fri L and D, Sat–Sun L; $

Frequently cited as the best place to get Cambodia's answer to the *banh mi*-style sandwich, this tiny shop (beware: no seats) was started by two veteran chefs who combine Cambodian flavors with French baguettes. The pulled pork and glazed pork belly sandwiches stand out, but the soups and salads are also bursting with distinct and fresh ingredients.

② GRAND CENTRAL OYSTER BAR & RESTAURANT
Grand Central Terminal (42nd Street and Park Avenue); tel: 212-490-6650; www.oysterbarny.com; Mon–Sat L and D; $$

Shellfish rules at this classic Gotham eatery in the vaulted lower level of Grand Central Terminal. Oysters and other bivalves are served on the half-shell, in chowder, in pan roasts, and in 'po'boy' sandwiches.

③ CIPRIANI DOLCI
Grand Central Terminal (42nd Street and Park Avenue); tel: 212-973-0999; www.cipriani.com; daily L and D; subway: Grand Central Terminal; $$$

Hearty Italian fare from the folks behind Venice's iconic Harry's Bar, on a balcony overlooking Grand Central Terminal's magnificent concourse.

④ THE CAMPBELL
Grand Central Terminal (42nd Street and Park Avenue); tel: 212-297-1781; www.thecampbellnyc.com; daily L and D; $$

Jazz Age business magnate John W. Campbell designed this office in the station in the 13th-century Florentine style and used it for work during the day and socializing in the evenings. Restored, it is now an elegant cocktail lounge.

⑤ P.J. CLARKE'S
915 Third Avenue (at 55th Street); tel: 212-317-1616; www.pjclarkes.com; daily L and D; $$

Pouring pints since 1884, one of the city's great saloons operates just as it has for many years, albeit with modern prices. It can be rowdy, but it's a classic.

Central Park's lake

CENTRAL PARK

The heart – some say the lungs – of Manhattan is a manmade recreation area that spans 51 blocks from 59th to 110th streets. The park covers 6 percent of Manhattan. The route below is relaxed, and a good one to do with children. Twenty-one playgrounds provide happy respites.

DISTANCE: 2 miles (3.5km)
TIME: A half-day
START: Grand Army Plaza
END: Central Park West
POINTS TO NOTE: This tour could be linked with a visit to the museum (route 6). Note that it is not advisable to wander the park at night. Check the park's website for details on free guided tours and audio tours.

Central Park (www.centralparknyc.org; daily 6am–1am) was laid out by landscape architects Frederick Law Olmsted and Calvert Vaux over almost 20 years, starting in 1858. Creating lush naturalistic parkland from a sparse, rocky landscape was an incredible achievement: almost everything here is manmade.

AROUND THE DAIRY

Enter the park at **Grand Army Plaza ❶** at Fifth Avenue and East 59th Street, where you will be confronted by Augustus Saint-Gaudens's huge gilded eques-trian statue of Civil War general William Tecumseh Sherman. A trail to the west leads along the edge of the Pond.

Continue north to the **Wollman Rink ❷**, used from October through April as an ice-skating rink (Mon–Tue 10am–2.30pm, Wed–Thu 10am–10pm, Fri–Sat 10am–11pm, Sun 10am–9pm) and the rest of the year as an amusement park. North of here is the **Dairy ❸**, built in 1870 to provide fresh milk and toys to city children. It is now a **visitor information center** (daily 10am–5pm). Check here for tours.

If you're doing the tour with children, take Transverse Road No. 1 west to the vintage **Carousel ❹**, then retrace your steps to the Dairy and follow the path east to the **Central Park Zoo ❺** (www.centralparkzoo.com; Apr–Oct Mon–Fri 10am–5pm, Sat–Sun 10am–5.30pm, Nov–Mar daily 10am–4.30pm), home of polar bears, sea lions, penguins, otters, and over 100 other animal species, and the nearby **Tisch Children's Zoo ❻**.

Return toward the Dairy, then head north across Transverse Road and Park

Strolling in the park

Winter ice–skating

Drive to **The Mall**, a formal promenade bordered by elm trees and statues of eminent writers.

AROUND THE LAKE

The Mall leads to **Bethesda Terrace ❼**, a two-level plaza overlooking the **Lake ❽** and the architectural center-piece of the park. On the lake's north-east end is the **Loeb Boathouse ❾**, where you can rent bicycles and row-boats or enjoy a chic meal in the park's main restaurant (see page 115).

From the boathouse, walk east, toward **Conservatory Water ❿**, on which model-boat enthusiasts sail radio-controlled miniature yachts. Note the statues: *Alice in Wonderland* to the north of the pond, and *Hans Christian Andersen* to the west.

THE RAMBLE AND NORTH

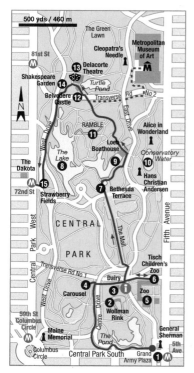

From here, explore the trails that lead through the wooded **Ramble ⓫** toward **Belvedere Castle ⓬**, which is the other side of Transverse Road No. 2. Perched atop a rock at the edge of **Turtle Pond**, this fanciful stone structure, designed in 1865 as a folly, is now a weather sta-tion and nature center. It was closed for renovations at the time of writing, but due to reopen in 2019.

Across Turtle Pond is the **Delacorte Theatre ⓭**, focus of the Public Theat-er's free 'Shakespeare in the Park' festival in the summer (www.shake-speareinthepark.org). The **Shake-speare Garden ⓮** features plants mentioned in the Bard's plays.

To exit the park, walk south along West Drive, stopping level with 72nd Street at **Strawberry Fields ⓯**, a small area dedicated to John Lennon, who was shot and killed outside **The Dakota** apartment building across from Central Park West in 1980.

The Met is home to over 2 million pieces

METROPOLITAN MUSEUM OF ART

The grande dame of New York's museums showcases more than 3 million works of art from across the continents and the ages. The scale is intimidating, so let this museum route guide you through the highlights.

DISTANCE: N/A – the whole tour is spent within the museum
TIME: A half-day
START/END: The Met
POINTS TO NOTE: Note that the Met is open late on Friday and Saturday. Free gallery talks and guided tours are offered daily. See www.metmuseum.org or stop at the information desk in the Great Hall, where you can also rent an audio guide.

This tour touches on some of the most popular collections of the **Metropolitan Museum of Art ❶** (1000 Fifth Avenue at 82nd Street; www.metmuseum.org; daily 10am–5.30pm, Fri–Sat until 9pm), one of New York's prime attractions, drawing over 5 million visitors each year.

Depending on your starting time, fortify yourself with brunch or lunch at **Sant Ambroeus ❶**, or, if the weather is particularly sunny, go for a picnic in Central Park, directly behind the museum. Alternatively, if you're keen

to get started, you could go for a quick bite at the museum's **Cafeteria ❷**, which also offers substantial dishes.

Background

The Met is a palatial gallery with a collection of paintings, sculpture, drawings, furnishings, and items of the decorative arts spanning 10,000 years of human creativity. Featuring works by artists from Bruegel to Botticelli to Van Gogh, it showcases works from nearly every civilization. Exhibits range from flints found in Egypt dating to the Lower Paleolithic period (300,000–75,000 BC) to 21st-century couture by the renowned late fashion designer Alexander McQueen.

The Met's collection was established in 1870 by a group of artists and enthusiasts who wanted an American gallery that would rival those in Europe. One of Central Park's architects, British-born Calvert Vaux, along with Jacob Wrey Mold, designed the museum's first permanent home. The current building has housed the collection since 1880, with its facade

The American Wing   *In the Greek and Roman Galleries*

remodeled in 1926. The institution owns over 2 million items, though only around a quarter of the total collection is on display at any one time in its nearly 250 rooms. Additions and gallery renovations are frequent, and the collection on display is always changing. No matter how many times you visit, it's always a new place.

FIRST FLOOR

Enter the museum and buy tickets at the aptly named **Great Hall**. The most sensible way to tour the museum is by moving in a counter-clockwise direction, so start with Egyptian art to the right of the Great Hall as you enter.

Ancient Egypt

The Met's holdings in the field of Ancient Egypt are excellent. Statues, figurines, funerary art, and coffins are

arranged chronologically in a series of rooms leading to the Temple of Dendur, a sandstone Nubian temple from 15 BC, dedicated to the goddess Isis, the god Osiris, and the sky god Horus, among others. Discovered around 50 miles (80km) south of Aswan, the temple had to be saved from submersion when the Aswan High Dam was built; it was presented to the United States by Egypt in 1965 in recognition of the former's help with saving other important monuments during the dam's construction.

American Wing

Behind the Egyptian rooms is the redone American Wing, which reopened in 2009 after substantial work. The multi-level collection includes furnished period rooms, a stunning loggia designed by Louis Comfort Tiffany for his Laurelton Hall home, balcony displays of ceramics, glass, pewter, art pottery, and silver from Paul Revere to Tiffany. The Charles Engelhard Court wows with 60 examples of large-scale sculpture, mosaics, and stained glass, including works by Daniel Chester French and Augustus St Gaudens.

Galleries of paintings are found on the second floor and showcase such iconic images as Emanuel Leutze's *Washington Crossing the Delaware* and Gilbert Stuart's *George Washington*, as well as works by Edward Hopper, James Abbott McNeill Whistler, and John Singer Sargent.

Peruvian Funerary mask

If you're ready for a break at this point, relax at the first floor **American Wing Café** ③, or the slightly more expensive **Petrie Court Café** ④, in the adjacent European Sculpture Court.

European art

Two floors of galleries are devoted to European sculpture, paintings, and decorative arts, plus richly appointed period rooms. The works are hung in roughly chronological fashion, starting with Giotto and his *Adoration of the Magi* (c.1320), followed by an unfolding of the Italian Renaissance, with highlights by Raphael, Botticelli, Tintoretto, Titian, and Veronese.

Farther along is Spanish art, showcasing the work of Velázquez, Goya, and El Greco. A section devoted to Dutch paintings includes pieces by Rembrandt and Johannes Vermeer, notably his *Young Woman with a Water Pitcher* (1662). The British Galleries, containing works like Thomas Gainsborough's *Boy with a Cat* (1787), were closed for renovations at the time of writing, due to reopen in 2020.

European paintings and sculpture of the 19th century are grouped together in a separate room on the second floor. Among the many Post-Impressionist works found here are Van Gogh's *Wheat Field with Cypresses*, which he painted while confined to an asylum in 1889, and Paul Gauguin's Edenic view of South Sea life, *La Orana Maria (Hail Mary)*.

Modern art

The Met defines 'modern art' as dating from the year 1900, and ranging over two floors in the back of the museum are exhibits depicting different artistic movements. Although the idea of Modernism was initially controversial (in one episode, a traditional trustee gave reluctant approval for a purchase by covering his eyes and murmuring, 'I just can't look'), the museum nevertheless compiled an impressive collection, including pieces by Picasso, Matisse, O'Keeffe, and de Kooning. Sculpture highlights include the elegant *Sleeping Muse* by Constantin Brancusi (1910), the ten-foot tall marble *Kouros* by Isamu Noguchi, and the Dada-inspired *Narva* by Jean Tinguely (1961).

Greek and Roman art

Completing the circular route are the single-level Greek and Roman Galleries, next to the Great Hall. These house the Met's extensive collection of artifacts dating from c.900 BC to the early 4th century AD, bringing under one roof the very foundations of Western artistic civilization.

SECOND FLOOR

The Arts of the Arab Lands, Turkey, Iran, Central Asia, and Later South

A full set of armor　　　　　　　　　　　*The Great Hall balconies*

Asia opened in 2011 and is one of the more ambitious expansions of the museum, with fifteen galleries highlighting Islamic art, textiles, sculpture, woodworking, earthenware, and arms. Don't forget to tilt your head back in the Koç Family Galleries and take in the majesty of the ornate 16th-century carved wooden ceiling.

The area to the right of the Great Hall's balcony contains a series of rooms showcasing Asia: exhibits from Korea, China, and South and Southeast Asia. Behind them are small rooms featuring Japanese art, plus the Met's excellent collection of musical instruments.

In season, from May until later fall, end this route with a well-earned drink at the **Cantor Rooftop Garden Bar** ⑤, which has superb views across Central Park with its backdrop of elegant skyscrapers engulfing the horizon. Or visit the museum store, which sells reproduction posters, jewelry, note cards, and an excellent selection of art books associated with the museum's exhibits.

Food and drink

① SANT AMBROEUS
1000 Madison Avenue (between 77th and 78th streets); tel: 212-570-2211; www.santambroeus.com; daily B, L, and D; $$
After visiting the museum, you can charge up your batteries with a shot of espresso, a focaccia or another light bite such as a fresh salad, and perhaps dessert at this Milanese café.

② THE CAFETERIA
Ground floor, Metropolitan Museum of Art; Sun–Thu 11am–4.30pm, Fri–Sat 11.30am–6pm; $
A self-service restaurant where hungry masses congregate for a quick bite or full meal from a range of sandwiches, salads, and a selection of hot entrees.

③ AMERICAN WING CAFÉ
First floor, American Wing, Metropolitan Museum of Art; Sun–Thu 10am–4.30pm, Fri–Sat until 8.15pm; $
Enjoy sandwiches, salads, desserts, snacks, or cocktails, with park views.

④ PETRIE COURT CAFÉ
First floor, Metropolitan Museum of Art; daily 11.30am–4.30pm; $$
The bistro fare is pricier than The Cafeteria, but the room boasts great Central Park views.

⑤ CANTOR ROOFTOP GARDEN BAR
Fifth floor, Metropolitan Museum of Art; May–late fall Sun–Thu 11am–4.30pm, Fri–Sat 11am–8.15pm; $
Order a glass of wine at the bar and enjoy the views of Central Park and the city skyline.

The Upper East Side borders Central Park

UPPER EAST SIDE MUSEUMS

Some of America's finest cultural treasures are housed in galleries on the stretch of Fifth Avenue between 82nd and 110th streets, dubbed 'Museum Mile.' South of here, still on the wealthy Upper East Side, you'll find contemporary art at the Met Breuer and European masterpieces at the Frick Collection.

DISTANCE: 2 miles (3km)
TIME: A half- to full day
START: The Africa Center (or El Museo del Barrio)
END: Frick Collection
POINTS TO NOTE: Check museum opening times before deciding on which day to do this route; most are closed at least one day a week, often Monday. A number open late on Fridays.

It would be completely exhausting to see all the museums described in this route in a single day, so the best policy is to choose concentrate on two or three, according to your taste. Here, we start with the northernmost museum and work southwards through the Upper East Side. Where a museum is noted as undergoing renovations or redevelopment, be sure to check the relevant website before visiting for updates on latest opening times and exhibits. This is particularly true for the first museum on our route

MUSEUM MILE

The Africa Center
The long gestating **The Africa Center ❶** (1280 Fifth Avenue at 110th Street; www.theafricacenter. org) has delayed its opening more than half a dozen times over the last few years. Let's hope it will be ready soon, because it promises to be one of the world's best places to discover the art and culture of Africa and the African diaspora.

El Museo del Barrio
El Museo del Barrio ❷ (1230 Fifth Avenue at 104th Street; www.elmuseo.org; Wed–Sat 11am–6pm, Sun noon–5pm) showcases the art and culture of Puerto Rico and Latin America. Its permanent collection of over 6,500 objects spanning more than 800 years of Latino art includes pre-Columbian Taíno artifacts, traditional arts, 20th-century drawings, paintings, sculptures, and installations, as well as prints, photography, documentary films, and video. Chang-

In the Neue Galerie

ing exhibits highlight artists both past and present, while special programs offer talks, films, and poetry readings.

Museum of the City of New York

Just one block south is the **Museum of the City of New York ❸** (1220 Fifth Avenue at 103rd Street; www.mcny.org; daily 10am–6pm), which chronicles the colorful story of New York from Dutch colonial times to the present. The collection encompasses myriad artifacts and artworks related to the city's ever-changing character and phenomenal growth, including historic paintings, vintage dollhouses, and much more.

Jewish Museum

Several blocks further on, the **Jewish Museum ❹** (1109 Fifth Avenue; www.thejewishmuseum.org; Sat–Tue 11am–5.45pm, Thu 11am–8pm, Fri 11am–4pm; free on Sat) is located in a fine French Renaissance-style mansion built *c*.1908. Inside is an excellent collection of Judaica: art, artifacts, photographs, and antiques that tell the story of Jewish persistence in an age-old struggle. The permanent and rotating exhibitions illuminate more than 4,000 years of Jewish cultural history, focusing on luminaries from across the arts such as Leonard Cohen, Marc Chagall, Martha Rosler and more.

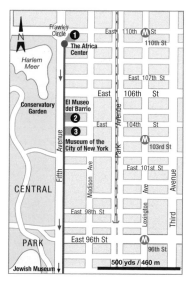

Museum Mile Festival

A highly popular fixture in the New York cultural calendar since its inception in the 1970s, the Museum Mile Festival (http://museummilefestival.org) is held on the second Tuesday in June from 6 to 9pm and regularly attracts a crowd of more than 50,000 art-lovers and fun-seekers. The whole of the Museum Mile, i.e. Fifth Avenue from the Metropolitan Museum north to El Museo del Barrio, is closed to traffic, and musicians, street performers, and food stalls line the route. All of the museums open for the evening, with special temporary exhibits also mounted to coincide with the festival.

The Cooper–Hewitt Smithsonian Design Museum store

An excellent option for brunch at this juncture is **Sarabeth's** ❶, on Madison, one block east along 92nd Street from the Jewish Museum.

Cooper-Hewitt Smithsonian Design Museum

Back on Fifth Avenue, the next museum when heading south is the **Cooper-Hewitt Smithsonian Design Museum** ❺ (2 East 91st Street; www.cooperhewitt.org; Sun–Fri 10am–6pm, Sat until 9pm), a branch of the Smithsonian Institution housed in steel magnate Andrew Carnegie's 1902 mansion. The museum has excellent collections of decorative and applied arts, as well as industrial design, fulfilling its original mission as a 'visual library' of the history of style.

National Academy Museum

About a block and a half farther along is the **National Academy Museum and School of Fine Arts** ❻ (1083 Fifth Avenue at 89th Street; www.nationalacademy.org; Wed–Sun 11am–6pm, hours change seasonally).

This is the country's oldest artist-run organization, founded in 1825 to train artists and show their work. It upholds the custom of members submitting a self-portrait and a representative example of their work: a tradition that fortifies the academy's collection of 2,200 paintings, 240 sculptures, and 5,000 works on paper.

Past members of the academy have included Frederic East Church, Winslow Homer, John Singer Sargent, and Jasper Johns.

The Guggenheim

Perhaps the greatest work of art at the **Solomon R. Guggenheim Museum** ❼ (1071 Fifth Avenue at

The National Academy

The Guggenheim's most famous feature

89th Street; www.guggenheim.org; Fri and Sun–Wed 10am–5.45pm, Sat until 7.45pm) is the building itself – architect Frank Lloyd Wright's landmark spiral design. At the core of the collection are the works of some of the leading artists since Modernism reared its head in the latter part of the 19th century. Many were associated with movements such as Expressionism, Cubism, and the trend toward abstraction; such painters as Klee, Kandinsky, Mondrian, Modigliani, Léger, Picasso, and Pollock. The museum houses a gourmet restaurant, the Wright (brunch and lunch only).

Neue Galerie

Three blocks south is the **Neue Galerie ❽** (1048 Fifth Avenue at 86th Street; www.neuegalerie.org; Thu–Mon 11am–6pm), in a splendid mansion built in 1912–14 by architects Carrère & Hastings, whose New York Public Library reflects the same French Beaux Arts-style influence.

The museum was founded by the son and heir of cosmetics giant Estée Lauder, Ron Lauder, a former US ambassador to Austria with an interest in Germanic art and sufficiently deep pockets to indulge his passion. His collection, much of which was amassed through the Madison Avenue gallery of Serge Sabarsky, focuses on 20th-century German and Austrian art, with works by Gustav Klimt, Egon Schiele, and various Bauhaus representatives. There are also some items of decorative arts.

The museum **café ❷**, named after Sabarsky, is an appropriately artful

The Guggenheim

Art at the Met Breuer

place to stop for a bite; Café Fledermaus, on the lower level, serves the same menu.

The Metropolitan Museum

The southernmost point of Museum Mile proper ends with the most renowned of the nine museums, the **Metropolitan Museum of Art** ❾ (1000 Fifth Avenue at 82th Street; www.metmuseum.org; Sun–Thu 10am–5.30pm, Fri and Sat 10am–9pm). As the museum is so vast – the largest in the United States – we devote an entire route to it (see page 50).

An option for food at this point is **Candle 79**, see ❸, accessed by turning left onto East 79th Street.

A pleasant adjunct to a museum visit is a stroll in the **Conservatory Garden** (daily 8am–dusk), a portion of Central Park at Fifth Avenue and 105th Street. Situated behind gates that once adorned one of the Vanderbilt mansions, this little-known oasis encompasses 6 acres (2 hectares) of manicured grounds divided into Italian, English, and French formal gardens. Guided tours are available Saturdays at 11am and Wednesdays at noon in the spring and summer.

BEYOND MUSEUM MILE

While in the mood for art, you may wish to visit the Met Breuer or the Frick Collection; both are within walking distance.

The brutalist building on the corner of Madison Avenue and 75th Street, designed by the modernist architect Marcel Breuer, was once the home of the Whitney Museum of American Art. This imposing structure now houses the **Met Breuer** ❿ (945 Madison Avenue at 75th Street; www.metmuseum.org/visit/met-breuer), an offshoot of the Metropolitan Art Museum dedicated to modern and contemporary art. The cantilevered structure is a work of art in its own right, second only to the Guggenheim among the Upper East Side's most striking architectural expressions. As well as providing space for 20th- and 21st-century masterpieces from the vast Met collection, the Met Breuer runs a varied program of exhibitions, events, and performances.

If you're hungry, try the nearby **Café Boulud** ❹, on East 76th Street.

Frick Collection

Return to Fifth Avenue and wrap up your tour five blocks south at the **Frick Collection** ⓫ (1 East 70th Street; www.frick.org; Tue–Sat 10am–6pm, last entry 5.30pm; Sun 11am–5pm, last entry 4.30pm), which occupies a mansion built in 1914 by steel magnate Henry Clay Frick. The building itself was constructed around a spectacular collection of art from the Renaissance through to the late 19th century. Intended from the beginning as a legacy to future generations, it

Gainsborough portraits at the Frick

remains one of the world's finest testaments to a connoisseur's vision.

The collection focuses on European paintings (including three Vermeers) and furnishings and represents one of the city's most successful combinations of art and environment. The ambience is one of quiet gentility. Leave plenty of time for the central courtyard, a soothing respite from the city streets.

Each year, the Frick's concert season showcases young classical musicians. Tickets must be booked in advance; see the website for dates of upcoming performances.

Roosevelt Island

For a little bit of outdoor adventure as a break from the museums, try visiting tiny **Roosevelt Island**, which parallels the Upper East Side. It has just one church, one supermarket, and lovely views of Manhattan's skyline, especially at sunset. The most enjoyable way to arrive is by the Roosevelt Island Tramway, which you can catch at Second Avenue and 60th Street near Bloomingdale's.

Food and drink

① SARABETH'S

1295 Madison Avenue (at 92nd Street); tel: 212-410-7335; www.sarabethsrestaurants. com; daily B, L, and D; $$
To-die-for muffins, pastries, and other baked goods as well as fluffy omelets and pancakes make this an ideal breakfast (or lunch) choice for museum patrons.

② CAFÉ SABARSKY

1048 Fifth Avenue (at 86th Street); tel: 212-288-0665; Mon and Wed B and L, Thu–Sun B, L, and D; $$$
In the paneled café on the Neue Galerie's ground floor, visitors can savor the dark coffee and excellent desserts of an old Viennese-style restaurant. Replicas of period banquettes and Bentwood furniture, plus a Josef Hoffmann chandelier, provide a setting that is luxurious and distinctive. A cabaret performance and prix-fixe dinner are presented at the café on selected Friday evenings.

③ CANDLE 79

154 East 79th Street; tel: 212-537-7179; www.candle79.com; daily L and D, Sat–Sun also Br; $$$
A stylish setting for sophisticated vegetarian and vegan dishes made from organic ingredients.

④ CAFÉ BOULUD

20 East 76th Street (near Madison Avenue); tel: 212-772-2600; www.cafeboulud.com; daily B, L, and D; $$$
Renowned French-born chef Daniel Boulud combines family and regional specialties with haute cuisine to create classic French dishes.

The Lincoln Center

UPPER WEST SIDE

A tour of the Natural History Museum's dinosaur collection and the Rose Center for Earth and Space, followed by a stroll down Columbus Avenue and a look around Lincoln Center, which offers opera, ballet, and theater, and the Time Warner Center, with shops, dining, and jazz performances.

DISTANCE: 1.25 miles (2km)
TIME: A full day
START: American Museum of Natural History
END: Time Warner Center
POINTS TO NOTE: The American Museum of Natural History is an excellent attraction for children and adults. The museum is vast, and we advise that you concentrate on two or three sections, perhaps punctuated with a film at the museum's Samuel J. and Ethel LeFrak Theater. You may wish to end the day with a performance or gig at the Lincoln Center or Time Warner Center.

The apartment buildings west of Central Park include some of the city's most distinctive, like the twin-towered San Remo, and the well-known, turreted Dakota (John Lennon was shot outside here). It's a neighborhood beloved by its residents. Part of this is the fact that the Upper West Side is within walking distance of three of New York's most popular attractions and some of its best food shopping.

You'll need lots of energy for this tour, so be sure to leave time for a good breakfast or brunch before starting. There are numerous restaurants in this part of town; two good options near our first stop are both northwest near 83rd Street: **Café Lalo** ❶, and **Good Enough to Eat** ❷. Alternatively, have an early lunch at the Natural History Museum's **Food Court** ❸.

AMERICAN MUSEUM OF NATURAL HISTORY

If you're traveling with children, one attraction that you shouldn't miss is the **American Museum of Natural History** ❶ (Central Park West at 79th Street; www.amnh.org; daily 10am–5.45pm), although there are millions of reasons for adults to visit, too. In fact, some 32 million: the estimated number of artifacts and specimens housed within the museum's 25 buildings, only 2 percent of which are on display at any given time. The museum is so huge that it would be impossible to

Tyrannosaurus rex

cover everything here; instead, we focus on some of the highlights.

Enter the museum via the main entrance on 79th Street; here, a statue of Theodore Roosevelt stands guard. Outside, the steps are a popular regrouping point, where families and school parties study their guidebooks and maps.

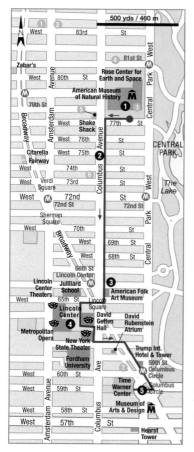

Background

Naturalist Dr Albert S. Bickmore had a passion for a natural history museum, and lobbied tirelessly for one to be established. In 1869 he succeeded in helping to found the museum, which began exhibiting its collections in Central Park's Arsenal building two years later. In 1874, US President Ulysses S. Grant laid the cornerstone for the museum's permanent home at 77th Street, although the original building was subsumed by later extensions that included a Romanesque Revival facade on 77th Street and the facade on Central Park West. At the northern end of the grounds is a glass cube housing the Rose Center for Earth and Space, which is dramatically lit at night.

Fourth-floor Orientation Center

If you only have time to see one part of the museum, head straight up to the fourth floor, home to the world's largest exhibition of dinosaur fossils. Start at the **Wallach Orientation Center**, where a film narrated by actress Meryl Streep explains the modern system of 'cladistics,' which organizes living things into an evolutionary family tree made up of a series of groups with shared anatomical features.

Brown bear diorama

Hall of Vertebrate Origins

Adjacent to the Orientation Center is the Hall of Vertebrate Origins. Here, the evolutionary tale starts about 500 million years ago. Massive armored fish such as the Dunkleosteus, whose head was encased in bony armor, appeared 360 million years ago and ruled the seas. Even more dramatic are such flying reptiles as pterosaurs and real-life sea monsters, including the ichthyosaurs.

Most terrifying of all is the fossilized jaw of a Carcharadon megaladon, a giant shark which roamed the seas 10 million years ago. These great animals reached up to 18 meters in length – that's three times the size of the biggest known great white – and are especially notable for their teeth, which grew to over half a foot in length.

Hall of Saurischian Dinosaurs

Just around the corner, the first of two popular dinosaur halls focuses on the saurischians, or 'lizard-hipped,' dinosaurs. In the center of the hall, representing the two major branches of the saurischian family, are the towering skeletons of **Tyrannosaurus rex** and **Apatosaurus**, both repositioned with tails held aloft for balance instead of dragging on the ground to reflect the contemporary view that they were agile creatures rather than the ponderous, tail-dragging behemoths that were envisioned by early paleontologists.

The Tyrannosaurus is composed of fossils from a T. rex found in Montana in 1902 and 1908. The broken ribs, damaged vertebra, and a facial abscess were possibly sustained in battles with other animals.

Next to T. rex, munching on the tail of a sauropod, is an Allosaurus. Other large theropods (two-legged, meat-eating dinosaurs) are exhibited in displays along the side wall.

At the opposite end of the hall is the world's only display of a fossil Deinonychus, an agile predator about the size of a human. It is shown in mid-leap, ready to rip into its prey with clawed hands and – deadliest of all – the sickle-like claw on the second toe of each foot.

Hall of Ornithiscian Dinosaurs

The next hall covers the ornithiscians, dinosaurs with backward-pointing hipbones. This group includes armored and horned dinosaurs such as Stegosaurus and Triceratops. Also here are duckbill dinosaurs, whose rows of flat teeth were designed for grinding plant matter. The most significant specimen here is the '**Dinosaur Mummy,**' an Edmontosaurus with rare soft tissue, including a patch of skin clearly covered with tubercles similar to those of a lizard or a bird's feet.

Early mammals

The next two halls on the fourth floor focus on **Primitive Mammals** and **Advanced Mammals**, emphasizing the diversity of the lineage. The forebears

Ostriches on display　　　　　　　　　　　　*Gemsbock dioramas*

of the mammalian line were anything but warm and fuzzy, a fact illustrated by the fossilized remains of Dimetrodon, a large lizard-like creature with a spiny sail on its back. More familiar fossils include those of prehistoric marsupials, giant glyptodonts, and an 8ft (2.5-meter) -tall ground sloth.

The last gallery is dominated by creatures that our Ice Age ancestors may have hunted (or been hunted by), including cave bears, saber-toothed cats, enormous rhino-like brontotheres with shovel-shaped prongs on their snouts, and mammoths with curled tusks.

Rose Center for Earth and Space

If time permits, head for another museum highlight: the **Rose Center for Earth and Space**. This state-of-the-art science center houses the **Hayden Planetarium**, an aluminum sphere 87ft (27 meters) in diameter. The planetarium is split into two theaters: in the upper half is the 429-seat, dome-screened Space Theater featuring the latest space show, *Dark Universe*, which launches visitors through space and time to experience the life and death of the stars in our night sky. The lower half houses the Big Bang exhibit, where viewers peer down at a basin-shaped screen onto which laser images trace the beginnings of the universe.

Spiraling down from the sphere is the Heilbrunn Cosmic Pathway, a dramatic ramp that ushers guests through 13 billion years of cosmic evolution. The pathway leads to the **Hall of the Universe**, a large exhibition space with displays on star formation, asteroid collisions, black holes, and other celestial phenomena. Near the center of the hall is the **Willamette Meteorite**, an eroded 15.5-ton hunk of nickel-iron forged in a distant star.

A stairway leads from the Hall of the Universe to the **Hall of Planet Earth**, which focuses on the geological forces that reshape the planet. Multimedia displays explore volcanism, plate tectonics, seismology, climatology, and other aspects of earth science.

Other highlights

Fortunately for interested but foot-weary visitors, other highlights are all situated on the first floor. Just to the left of the Theodore Roosevelt Memorial Hall is the beautifully designed **Hall of Biodiversity**, a celebration of the planet's life forms and a call for their protection. The 100ft (30-meter) -long *Spectrum of Life* is an array of more than 1,500 models and specimens, evoking the glorious variety of life on earth. Other displays focus on endangered species and contemporary issues such as global warming, deforestation, and habitat loss.

To the left of Café on One by the 77th Street entrance is the **Hall of Human Origins**, where exhibits tell the story of Homo sapiens, beginning with apelike australopithecines to the fully human people of Ice Age Europe. On display

Costa Rican stone sculptures

are casts of a 3.5 million-year-old Australopithecus afarensis couple walking across the plain and 1.6 million-year-old Turkana Boy (Homo ergaster).

Fans of famous gemstones should head for the **Morgan Memorial Hall of Gems** on the first floor of the museum (closed for renovations at the time of writing, but due to reopen in fall 2019). Highlights include the dazzling 563-carat Star of India sapphire, donated to the museum in 1900, and the Patricia Emerald, a 632-carat uncut beauty.

Don't forget to visit the renovated **Theodore Roosevelt Memorial Hall**

with its four scenic dioramas; these pay tribute to the American president who was a pioneer in the conservation movement and had long been a supporter of this museum.

Samuel J. and Ethel LeFrak Theater

After such a long tour of what are just the highlights, you may be ready for a rest in the spacious **Samuel J. and Ethel LeFrak Theater**, which is situated directly in the middle of the first floor. 3D and 2D films, usually with natural history themes and occasionally featuring museum staff on fact-finding expeditions, are screened throughout the day.

COLUMBUS AVENUE

Upon leaving the museum, consider a stroll along **Columbus Avenue** ❷, which runs north–south directly behind. The avenue and adjacent neighborhood are home to designer boutiques as well as numerous enticing restaurants and bars, including (from north to south) **Calle Ocho**, **Café Frida**, and **Alice's Tea Cup**, see ❹, ❺, and ❻, so take a break here if your feet are in need of rest. Just before hitting the intersection with Broadway, you'll come across **The American Folk Art Museum** ❸ (2 Lincoln Square at West 66th Street; www.folkartmuseum.org; Mon–Thu and Sat 11.30am–7pm, Fri noon–7.30pm, Sun noon–6pm), an important and delightful collection of

Detour for food-lovers

To see the remarkable gigantic food markets of the Upper West Side, detour two blocks west to Broadway. Zabar's, at 80th Street, is a city institution founded in 1934 and packed to the gills with cheeses, meats, coffees, and prepared foods to go. Walk south to 75th Street and Citarella, which boasts the largest seafood selection in the city, artfully displayed like fine jewels, plus gourmet groceries, pastry, and produce. Fairway Market occupies the entire block between 74 and 73rd streets, with produce stands lining the sidewalk outside and floor-to-ceiling displays within of every imaginable kind of food. By now you will no doubt be hungry, and both Zabar's and Fairway are ready to help with their own cafés.

Hayden Planetarium   *An Aztec sun stone*

pieces by self-taught artists from the 18th century through today.

If you're visiting the museum on Sunday, be sure to leave time to browse the weekly **Green Flea Market** (www.greenfleamarkets.com; Sun 10am–5.30pm) on Columbus Avenue between West 76th and 77th streets, where scores of vendors sell crafts, antiques, vintage clothes, and other household items, as well as fresh produce and baked goods.

If you wonder why there are long lines at the corner of Columbus and 77th Street, they are for the juicy, thick Black Angus beef hamburgers at **Shake Shack** (www.shakeshack.com; daily L and D; $). Begun as a stand in Madison Square Park, the wildly popular chain, which also serves hot dogs, shakes, and custard, now has locations across the country and internationally. It doesn't hurt that the prices are a rare bargain.

LINCOLN CENTER

Once you've eaten enough or spent enough, continue south down Columbus Avenue to 65th Street, where Broadway also swerves to meet you. On your right is the **Lincoln Center for the Performing Arts** ❹ (guided tours every 2 hours daily, tel: 212-875-5456 for general enquiries; see www.lincoln-center.org for performance schedules, ticket information, and links to all the venues), where some 5 million peo-

ple a year enjoy classical music, ballet, theater, and film. It is fresh from a multimillion-dollar renovation that includes a new half-price ticket booth across the street.

In the 1950s, when the city needed a new opera house and a new home for the Philharmonic, situating them within the same complex was a far-sighted idea. So was erecting a sophisticated cultural center in this part of Manhattan, best known for drug-infested 'Needle Park,' and as the location for composer Leonard Bernstein's story of gang warfare, *West Side Story*. Today, of course, this is New York's premier arts center.

The spouting fountain in the middle of the central Josie Robertson Plaza is surrounded by the glass-and-white-marble facades of Lincoln Center's three main structures. The prestigious **Metropolitan Opera** is directly in front, with two large murals by Marc Chagall behind the glass wall.

Music and dance

To the left of the central fountain, the **David H. Koch Theater** is where the New York City Ballet takes the stage. The third side of the plaza is occupied by **David Geffen Hall**, home of the New York Philharmonic and the 'Mostly Mozart' summer concert series.

Behind David Geffen Hall (next to the Met) is a shady plaza and reflecting pool around which office workers gather for lunch. The bronze sculp-

Jazz at Lincoln Center

ture in the center of the pool is *Reclining Figure* by Henry Moore; set back from the plaza is the **Lincoln Center Theater**. Also within the complex are the distinguished **Juilliard School of Music**, the **Walter Reade Theater** for film, and the **Alice Tully Recital Hall**.

Building green

The greening of Manhattan has begun. The city's first fully certified green building is Hearst Tower, just south of Columbus Circle on Eighth Avenue between 57th and 56th streets, the headquarters of the publishing giant whose magazines include *Esquire*, *Cosmopolitan*, and *House Beautiful*. Designed by Sir Norman Foster and constructed atop the 1928 Art Deco Hearst building, the 46-story glass tower is designed to minimize waste and save energy. More than 90 percent of the tower's structural steel contains recycled material, as do the carpeting and furniture. A water collection system diverts rainwater to the air conditioners as well as to the three-story waterfall that cools the atrium. Sensors dim the lights when no one is present, and the tower's glass skin lets in sunlight without unwanted heat. Thanks to improved ventilation, air quality inside the building may be better than outside, which, in smoggy Midtown, leaves everyone breathing easier.

COLUMBUS CIRCLE

From Lincoln Center walk south down Broadway to the southwestern corner of Central Park toward **Columbus Circle ❺**.

On the north side of Columbus Circle is the Trump International Hotel and Tower, situated across from the gateway to Central Park. On the south side, look for the **Museum of Arts and Design** (www.madmuseum.org; Tue–Sun 10am–6pm, Thu until 9pm) in a distinctive building clad with terracotta panels. MAD, as it refers to itself, is dedicated to showing contemporary works in glass, metal, clay, wood, and paper.

Looming above and almost dwarfing Columbus Circle is the **Time Warner Center**, whose asymmetric glass towers look over the stately statue of explorer Christopher Columbus, for which the circle is named. The upscale stores and restaurants here played a key role in the recent regeneration of this area. The studios of TV channel CNN are on the third floor.

If it feels like time to refuel, stop off at **Bouchon Bakery and Café ❼** on the third floor of 10 Columbus Circus.

The Time Warner Center is also the home of **Jazz at Lincoln Center** (www.jazz.org), with two auditoriums. Visit the **Jazz Hall of Fame**, or perhaps end the day with a gig in the center's **Frederick P. Rose Hall** or cabaret in the Appel Room, accompanied with a dazzling city view through the back wall of glass.

The lobby of the Trump International Hotel and Tower

Food and drink

① CAFÉ LALO

201 West 83rd Street (at Amsterdam Avenue); tel: 212-496-6031; www.cafelalo. com; daily B, Br, L, and D; $

A hearty brunch is served daily until 4pm at this appealing café, while the all-day menu features hearty pastrami sandwiches, Moroccan eggs and fresh salads, to name just a few dishes. The bar stays open until late.

② GOOD ENOUGH TO EAT

520 Columbus Avenue (at W 85th Street); tel: 212-496-0163; www.goodenoughtoeat. com; daily B, L, and D; $

Meat loaf, pork roast, home-baked pies: comfort favorites are prepared to perfection and served in Americana-filled surroundings. The morning rush for muffins and pancakes is worth the wait.

③ MUSEUM FOOD COURT

American Museum of Natural History, lower level; daily 11am–4.45pm; $

The food at the largest restaurant in the complex is several cuts above typical museum fare, with fresh salads, sandwiches, grilled specialties, stone-oven pizzas, and an appealing choice of sweets. The barbecue and ethnic dishes are particularly tasty.

④ CALLE OCHO

45 West 81st Street (in the Excelsior Hotel); tel: 212-873-5025; www.calleochonyc.com; Mon–Fri D, Sat–Sun Br and D; $$

Fans say the mojitos at this sexy Caribbean lounge and restaurant are the city's best. Soft multicolored lights create an alluring, grotto-like atmosphere in the bar, which is a second home to many of the neighborhood's monied young professionals.

⑤ CAFÉ FRIDA

368 Columbus Avenue (near 77th Street); tel: 212-712-2929; www.cafefrida.com; Mon–Fri L and D, Sat–Sun Br, L, and D; $$$

Mexican favorites including enchiladas and fajitas are just the start at this friendly eatery. It also excels in less familiar regional specialties such as braised chicken in black mole sauce, tangy lamb, and seafood.

⑥ ALICE'S TEA CUP

102 West 73rd Street (at Columbus Avenue); tel: 212-799-3006; www.alicesteacup.com; daily B, Br, L, and D; $

A hundred types of tea and a dash of whimsy make this a lovely place for a light lunch and a heart to heart.

⑦ BOUCHON BAKERY AND CAFÉ

10 Columbus Circle (near 60th Street), Third Floor; tel: 212-823-9366; www. thomaskeller.com; daily B, L, and early D, Sat–Sun also Br; $

Thomas Keller opened this informal spot to bake the bread for his five-star restaurant, Per Se, and to offer coffees, salads, sandwiches, and quiche, as well as sumptuous desserts.

Two names for Lenox Avenue

HARLEM

America's largest and most famous African–American community continues to enjoy a renaissance, while retaining the heritage, jazz, gospel, and soul food that make a visit special.

> **DISTANCE:** 1.5 miles (2.5km)
> **TIME:** A half-day
> **START:** 135th Street subway
> **END:** Shabazz Market, 116th Street
> **POINTS TO NOTE:** Take the C train to 135th Street and Frederick Douglass Boulevard to start the route. The No. M7 bus runs along Lenox Avenue in both directions.

Harlem's history goes from Dutch settlement to upscale residential area to mecca for African-Americans. Writers like Langston Hughes, musicians, and artists made the area famous in the late 1920s, the era known as the Harlem Renaissance. Decades of lean years followed, but recent arrivals – attracted by the history and property prices – are changing the face of the neighborhood, although the flavor of old remains.

STRIVERS' ROW

From the 135th Street subway stop on Frederick Douglass Boulevard, walk north to 139th Street and turn right for the St Nicholas Historic District, two blocks of townhouses built in 1891, at the height of Harlem's residential boom. Loop up West 139th and down West 138th between Adam Clayton Powell Jr and Frederick Douglass boulevards to see the architecture. Prominent blacks attracted here account for the nickname **Strivers' Row ❶**.

On the corner of 138th Street and Adam Clayton Powell Jr Boulevard is the impressive stone **Abyssinian Baptist Church ❷** (https://abyssinian.org), one of the oldest and most influential congregations in the city. On Sunday mornings at 9am and 11.30am, all are welcome to join the throng waiting to hear the magnificent choir.

Continue on 138th Street to Lenox Avenue and turn right to 135th Street and the **Schomburg Center for Research in Black Culture ❸** (515 Lenox Avenue; www.schomburgcenter.org; Mon–Sat 10am–6pm, Tue–Wed until 8pm). A branch of the New York Public Library, this is part museum, part cultural center, and

Strivers' Row   *The Apollo Theater*

holds the nation's largest repository of black history and artifacts.

ART AND MUSIC

For soul food en route down Lenox Avenue, try **Sylvia's** (see page 115). Continue on to 127th Street and turn right to the commercial heart of Harlem. You'll see the changes taking place as well as the sidewalk vendors and small shops of old. Visit the **Studio Museum in Harlem** ❹ (429 West 127th Street; www.studiomuseum.org; Thu–Sun noon–6pm) to see work by contemporary black artists. The gallery is due to relocate to a new museum, on the site of the original at 144 West 125th Street, in 2021.

Turn back on yourself then right down Morningside Avenue, then left onto 125th Street where you'll find the **Apollo Theater** ❺ (253 West 125th Street; www.apollotheater.org), instrumental in the careers of Ella Fitzgerald and Stevie Wonder.

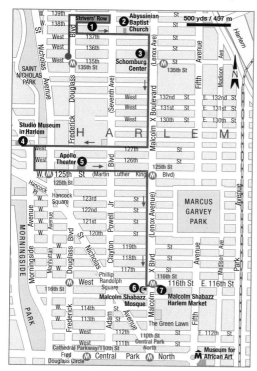

SHABAZZ MOSQUE AND MARKET

Continue to the hub of Harlem's Islamic community, marked by the green domed roof of the **Malcolm Shabazz Mosque** ❻ on Lenox Avenue, where Malcolm X once worshipped and preached. Turn east on 116th Street for a unique shopping stop, the **Malcolm Shabazz Harlem Market** ❼ (daily 10am–8pm). Past the gates of miniature minarets are stalls selling African art, drums, masks, and clothing.

THE CLOISTERS

Far from the hustle of Midtown Manhattan is this repository of medieval culture, set in a complex of reconstructed monasteries and curated by the Metropolitan Museum of Art.

DISTANCE: N/A – the whole tour is spent within The Cloisters
TIME: A half-day
START/END: The Cloisters
POINTS TO NOTE: Take the M4 bus to the last stop (Fort Tryon Park–The Cloisters). Or, if you don't mind a short walk, take the A train to 190th Street, exit by elevator, and walk north on Margaret Corbin Drive for 10 minutes.

If the city's frenetic pace is getting on your nerves, consider a serene journey to **The Cloisters** ❶ (Fort Tryon Park; www.metmuseum.org; Mar–Oct daily 10am–5.15pm, Nov–Feb daily 10am–4.45pm; staff guided tours available). Perched on a rocky bluff overlooking the Hudson River at Manhattan's northern tip, this branch of the Met is dedicated to medieval art and architecture. Much of the building is reconstructed from pieces of 12th-century monasteries.

The financial force behind the institution, as with so many others in New York, was John D. Rockefeller, Jr. But the man who was responsible for the treasures on display here was George Grey Barnard, a sculptor and collector who scoured the French countryside for church sculpture and architectural fragments. The result is that The Cloisters is an enchanting composite that evokes the hushed atmosphere of an ecclesiastical retreat. It's tranquil, fascinating, and as far away from the city as you can get without leaving Manhattan.

UPPER LEVEL

The Cloisters is on two levels. On the **upper level**, the *Unicorn Tapestries*, woven in Brussels in about 1500, have long been seen as the crown jewels of the museum's collection. The images depict the hunt of the mythological unicorn, whose capture, death, and restoration may represent the incarnation, death, and resurrection of Jesus Christ.

Three of the five cloisters are also on this floor. Directly in front of the room containing the *Unicorn Tapestries* is the **Cuxa Cloister**, from a Benedictine monastery in southern France. The Romanesque mar-

The garden at the Cloisters

ble capitals on the columns are characterized by intricately carved scrolling leaves, acanthus blossoms, and animals with two bodies and a common head. A fountain in the center of the enclosed garden divides the space into four grassy quadrants, each with a fruit tree and bordered by herbs and flowers.

Romanesque Hall

Separating two of the cloisters is the **Romanesque Hall**. Visitors enter through a massive rounded arch supported by huge limestone blocks. Crafted around 1150, the arch's capitals are carved in low relief with floral and animal motifs. Across from this entrance is a mid-13th-century pointed Gothic archway from the Burgundian monastery of Moutiers-St-Jean. A third doorway, the late 12th-century

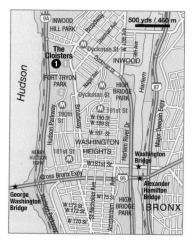

Reugny Door from the Loire Valley, has a pointed, recessed arch.

There are two chapels off the hall. Under the altar canopy in **Langon Chapel** is a wooden sculpture of the Virgin and Child. The **Fuentidueña Chapel**, with its imposing rounded apse, was originally a part of the church of San Martín in the Spanish village of Fuentidueña, north of Madrid.

Parallel to the Fuentidueña Chapel is the French **Saint-Guilhem Cloister**, which is from the Benedictine abbey of St-Guilhem-le-Désert, founded in 804 in southern France.

Pontaut Chapter House

Leading off the Cuxa Cloister are several impressive rooms. Just to the left is a reconstruction of the **Pontaut Chapter House** from Notre-Dame-de-Pontaut, a 12th-century abbey in southwestern France.

Walking in a counter clockwise direction leads to the **Early Gothic Hall,** where the stained-glass windows are superb examples of the new style that was succeeding the Romanesque in churches throughout Europe in the 12th century. Statuary displayed here includes the sandstone *Virgin* (*c*.1250) from the cathedral in Strasbourg, and the limestone *Virgin and Child* from the Ile-de-France of the mid-14th century.

In the next room are fragments of the Nine Heroes Tapestries, part of a 15th-century series of French pictorial textiles. The subjects of the tapestries are

Stained glass depicting a scene from the Ephesus legend

heroes from pagan, Hebrew, and Christian history and mythology.

Boppard and Campin Rooms

The **Boppard Room** contains ornate canopies with intricate twisting arches and leafy ornaments that frame six late Gothic stained-glass panels originally installed in a church at Boppard am Rhine. Adjacent, in the **Campin Room**, secular and religious themes are blended by 15th-century painter Robert Campin in his three-paneled Altarpiece of the Annunciation.

The Merode Room leads to the **Late Gothic Hall**. Sculptures dating from the latter part of the 15th century represent the Magi who visited Jesus after his birth. Parallel to the Late Gothic Hall is the third cloister, the **Froville Arcade**, built around nine pointed arches from a Benedictine priory.

LOWER LEVEL

Stairs from the upper level lead down to the **Glass Gallery**, where stained glass, sculpture, and tapestries are representative of late medieval works created for the burgeoning class of wealthy merchants and tradesmen, as well as for churches.

In the Glass Gallery are doorways leading to the other two cloisters. The **Trie-en-Bigorre Cloister** displays ornate carved capitals from the Carmelite convent and other religious orders in the Bigorre region of south-western France, as well as from monasteries near Toulouse. If you're feeling hungry at this point, the **Trie Café** ① is open from May to October.

Next door, the larger, late 13th- or early 14th-century **Bonnefont Cloister** has capitals and columns extracted from the Cistercian abbey at Bonnefont-en-Comminges. The simplicity of the capitals here is indicative of the strict asceticism of the monks, who considered ornamentation a distraction from the contemplation of God.

Gothic Chapel

The final room is the **Gothic Chapel**, where the effigy of crusader knight Jean d'Alluye lies upon his tomb. There are several stained-glass windows in this chapel, as well as funerary monuments, including the tombs of the Spanish counts of Urgell.

Stroll through Fort Tryon Park to the **New Leaf Restaurant & Bar** ②.

Food and drink

① TRIE CAFÉ

The Cloisters; May–Oct Tue–Sun L; $

Visitors can enjoy coffee, sweets, salads and sandwiches at a café in the walkway of a French cloister.

② NEW LEAF RESTAURANT & BAR

Fort Tryon Park; tel: 212-568-5323; Tue L, Wed–Fri L and D, Sat–Sun Br, L, and D; $$

At the southern entrance to Fort Tryon Park is this airy, oak-paneled café in a restored 1930s building, which turns out creative salads, sandwiches, and beef and chicken dishes. Live jazz on some Friday nights.

The Flatiron area from above

FLATIRON, SOFI, UNION SQUARE, AND CHELSEA

This route takes in some of Downtown's most innovative neighborhoods and sights: New York's first skyscraper, the Flatiron Building, buzzy Union Square, and artistic Chelsea.

> **DISTANCE:** 2.5 miles (4km)
> **TIME:** A half-day
> **START:** Flatiron Building
> **END:** Hotel Chelsea
> **POINTS TO NOTE:** The best days for this tour are Monday, Wednesday, Friday, or Saturday, when farmers come to Union Square for the Greenmarket. Note that most of Chelsea's galleries close on Monday.

Start this low-key, low-rise route at the corner of 23rd Street and Fifth Avenue. Fuel up on espresso or fortify yourself with some imported delicacies from the massive Italian food market **Eataly** ❶ (www.eataly.com). Then continue on to the east side of Broadway at 23rd Street by the Fuller Building, which is better known as the **Flatiron Building** ❶ because of its distinctive triangular shape.

Designed by renowned Chicago architect Daniel Burnham for the awkwardly shaped plot of land dividing Broadway and Fifth Avenue at 23rd, and constructed in 1902, the 285ft (87-meter) edifice was the first of the city's steel-frame skyscrapers and for a short time the tallest building in the world.

Rising 22 stories, the Flatiron was immortalized in 1903 in a classic black-and-white shot by the American Modernist photographer Alfred Stieglitz, who described it as looking 'like a monster steamer.'

SOFI

This neighborhood is commonly known as the Flatiron District, home to publishers and myriad small offices. Head south along Broadway – it's a 10-minute walk to Union Square – following a stretch once known as the 'Ladies Mile' that in the latter part of the 19th century ranged along Broadway and Sixth Avenue, from 23rd Street down to 9th Street. It is named for the number of fine department stores that operated here at that time; today, modern chains uphold the fashion tradition.

Union Square Greenmarket

Theodore Roosevelt Birthplace

On the walk to Union Square, you can make a left turn onto East 20th Street, and dip into the Gramercy neighborhood to visit the **Theodore Roosevelt Birthplace** ❷ (No. 28; www.nps.gov/thrb; Wed–Sun 9am–5pm, tours hourly 10am–4pm), a 1920s replica of the brownstone where the 26th US president was born in 1858 and spent his boyhood. After his death in 1919 it was rebuilt and rooms were recreated to show how a wealthy family such as the Roosevelts would have lived in the mid-19th century.

UNION SQUARE

A little farther south is **Union Square** ❸, named for its location at the busy convergence of Broadway and Fourth Avenue. This was a stylish area in the mid-1850s but was abandoned by the genteel set by the turn of the century. The square was notorious in the years before World War I as a platform for political demonstrations. Rallies drew crowds through the 1930s, but the lure of radicalism dwindled, and the area went into a long decline.

However, today's Union Square brims with life, a resurgence attributable in no small degree to the **Greenmarket** (Mon, Wed, Fri, Sat 8am–6pm), the biggest and best of the city's farmers' markets, held four days a week at the square's northern end (see box).

Adding to the regeneration has been the influx of publishers, advertising agencies, and other fashionable media firms into the area. The Union Square Partnership supplies the park with free Wi-Fi, and Manhattanites can be seen tapping on laptops and

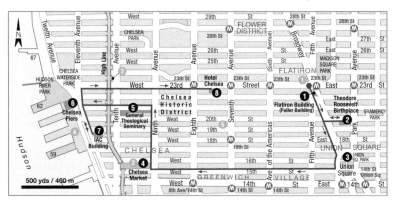

In Chelsea Market

mobile devices as they relax on the park's crowded benches.

CHELSEA

To the west of Union Square (from 14th up to about 20th Street) is fun, sophisticated, and arty Chelsea, a favorite neighborhood of New York's gay population. It is a mix of commercial streets and leafy residential areas. Eighth Avenue is a hub for dining, especially near the Joyce Theater (175 Eighth Avenue; www.joyce.org), an important showcase for modern dance troupes. Walk west to Ninth Avenue and you'll come to **Chelsea Market** ❹ (75 Ninth Avenue, 15th to 16th streets; www.chelseamarket.com; Mon–Sat 7am–2am, Sun 8am–10pm). An ambitious renovation transformed what were 18 buildings erected between 1883 and 1930 as a Nabisco bakery turning out Saltines and Oreos into a fantastic indoor market, with shops, restaurants and bars open late into the night. Much of the original brickwork and steel remain. The interior has a waterfall and sculptured seating, around which are gourmet shops, stores, and informal restaurants, such as **Hale and Hearty Soups** ❷.

Chelsea Historic District

After looking around the market, walk north on Ninth Avenue into the **Chelsea Historic District**, which

stretches between Eighth and Tenth avenues from 19th to 23rd streets. The land was inherited in 1813 by Clement Clarke Moore, then sold, with restrictions on development that have helped to preserve its elegant architecture. Moore is famed for writing *A*

The Greenmarket

If you were to ask celebrity chefs with restaurants near Union Square Park where they buy their ingredients, many could simply point out the window to the patches of concrete and the farm stands that are set up every Monday, Wednesday, Friday, and Saturday. The Union Square Greenmarket is more than a place to find apples in the fall and peaches in the summer. It is a community meeting place and essential source of produce for many New Yorkers, including those who make a living out of making meals.

Organic, and often exotic, meats are available alongside hand-tied pretzels and goat's cheese. In peak seasons, as many as 140 vendors will be offering their products, and the variety is astounding. In summer, you can easily find supplies for a gourmet picnic, including wine, artisan bread and homemade jams. Some of those celebrity chefs who shop at the market also do cooking demonstrations there. For more information visit www.grownyc.org.

The IAC Building

Visit from St Nicholas, which became the modern-day *'Twas the Night Before Christmas*.

On 21st Street between Ninth and Tenth avenues look for the main entrance to the 19th-century **General Theological Seminary** ❺ (440 West 21st Street; www.gts.edu; Mon–Fri 9am–5pm), the first seminary of the Episcopal Church. Register at the information desk, pick up a free walking tour pamphlet, and pass into an attractive tree-lined quadrangle that shelters buildings including the Chapel of the Good Shepherd and the former St Mark's Library.

Gallery-hopping

The boundaries of the Chelsea Gallery District have expanded enormously since this former industrial area first shook off its dusty image in the 1980s. It now extends roughly from 18th to 27th streets, mostly between Tenth and Eleventh avenues. Galleries are in quarters on the street or stacked up in vertical malls, where the elevator opens to a different gallery on each floor. The website http://chelseagallerymap.com contains lists of galleries and shows. The most sociable time of year is between September and December, when it's not uncommon for the area to play host to up to six receptions on the same night. Most galleries are closed Sun–Mon.

Gallery district

When you've completed your tour of the seminary, continue up Ninth Avenue, turn left at 22nd Street, and cross under the High Line for the heart of the area's gallery district. When priced out of Soho in the 1980s and 1990s, many art dealers began moving to this former industrial neighborhood, between Tenth and Eleventh avenues. Rising property prices have forced some galleries to relocate, but happily some still survive. The area is still famous for good restaurants such as **The Red Cat** ❸.

Chelsea Piers

If you prefer sport to art, stop by **Chelsea Piers** ❻, west across Eleventh Avenue. Until 1930 this waterfront served the Cunard and Star lines. After decades of neglect it has been reborn as a sports-and-entertainment complex stretching from 23rd to 17th streets, with roller rinks, ice rinks, a driving range, bowling alleys, batting cages, and a climbing wall. Dinner, wine-tasting and music cruises are available at the marina; in summer, the **Pier 66 Maritime Bar & Grill** ❹ is the perfect place for sunsets. The restored lightship, *Frying Pan*, docked alongside Pier 66 is worth a look, too.

IAC Building

Across Eleventh Avenue at 18th Street you can't miss the glass-clad **IAC Building** ❼. Designed by architect Frank Gehry, the curvy, sail-like form was inspired by his love of boats.

Outside the iconic Hotel Chelsea

Chelsea Hotel

Head up Eleventh Avenue and turn right onto 23rd Street. Between Eighth and Seventh avenues is **Hotel Chelsea** ❽ (222 West 23rd Street), a landmark of bohemian decadence and the second home of Beat poets, Warhol drag queens, and strung-out rock stars.

This is where poet Dylan Thomas was staying when he died in 1953; where Andy Warhol filmed *Chelsea Girls* in 1966; and where punk rocker Sid Vicious allegedly murdered his girlfriend Nancy Spungen in 1978 before dying of a drugs overdose.

The hotel has been under renovation for years and if/when it reopens, it certainly won't retain that grungy grandeur of old, but for a time-traveling experience, head down Seventh Avenue for dinner or a drink at **Peter McManus Café** ❺.

Food and drink

❶ EATALY

200 Fifth Avenue (at 23rd Street); tel: 212-229-2560; www.eataly.com; daily B, L, and D; $–$$$

From Mario Batali and the Bastianich family comes a multi-storied marketplace and food court with cheese, pizza, beer, panini, pasta, espresso, gelato, and every other Italian delicacy you can imagine.

❷ HALE AND HEARTY SOUPS

Chelsea Market, 75 Ninth Avenue; tel: 212-255 2443; www.haleandhearty.com; daily B, L, and D; $

Nothing hits the spot on a cold day like a steaming bowl of thick, flavorful soup and a slab of sourdough or seven-grain bread at this busy spot.

❸ THE RED CAT

227 Tenth Avenue (between 23rd and 24th streets); tel: 212-242-1122; www.theredcat. com; daily L and D; Sat–Sun also Br; $$

Gallery-hoppers gather at this welcoming, art-filled café in the heart of Chelsea's gallery district. The innovative New American chef does good things with classics like roast chicken or Atlantic salmon.

❹ PIER 66 MARITIME BAR & GRILL

Pier 66 in Hudson River Park, (entry from W 26th Street); tel: 212-989-6363; http://pier66maritime.com; May–Oct only, daily L and D; $$

A great spot for a drink with fine views across the river. It's a nice place to eat too, with an array of salads, seafood, and burgers on the menu.

❺ PETER MCMANUS CAFÉ

226 West 23rd Street (between Seventh and Eighth avenues); tel: 212-929-6196; www.petermcmanuscafe.com; daily L and D; $$

One of the oldest family-run restaurants in New York, this Irish pub has been serving steaks, burgers and beers since 1936.

Washington Square Park hosts many events

GREENWICH VILLAGE

A walking tour of notable sights, shops, bars, and cafés in what was once North America's foremost bohemian neighborhood, plus a foray into the trendy precincts of the Meatpacking District.

DISTANCE: 2.5 miles (4km)
TIME: A half- to full day
START: Intersection of Bleecker and MacDougal streets
END: West 14th Street and Tenth Avenue
POINTS TO NOTE: West 4th Street/Washington Square is the closest subway station to the starting point. Head south a few blocks along Sixth Avenue to reach Bleecker Street.

Start this walking tour near the intersection of Bleecker and MacDougal streets. **Caffe Reggio** ①, is one of the last of the classic cafés where you can sip coffee at a sidewalk table and recall bygone days, when artists, anarchists, and advocates of free love ranging from Edna St Vincent Millay and e. e. cummings to Jackson Pollock, Jack Kerouac, and Bob Dylan made 'the Village' the epicenter of New York's bohemian culture. Alternatively, head west up Bleecker and turn right onto Cordelia Street for superb seafood at **Pearl Oyster Bar** ②.

WASHINGTON SQUARE

Walk three blocks up MacDougal Street to **Washington Square Park** ①. Originally a potter's field and gathering place for public hangings, the park later became the residential center of the well-to-do New Yorkers portrayed in Henry James's classic novel *Washington Square*.

A colorful history is buried beneath the layers of concrete – at one time it served as a graveyard for the indigent and unknown. In 1888, Mark Twain took a train from Connecticut to meet Robert Louis Stevenson and they sat on the park benches discussing the writerly life, a moment immortalized by artist Francis Luis Mora. On the same benches is where, according to his autobiography, Marlon Brando first got drunk and passed out. A group of concerned citizens including Eleanor Roosevelt, who lived on Washington Square West, successfully campaigned to have car traffic removed from the park.

Nowadays the park serves variously as a town square, performance space,

Greenwich apartments	*Life imitating art in the West Village*

and unofficial campus for New York University, which owns most of the large modern buildings around the edges. Its everyday mix of students, chess hustlers, tourists, and carriage-pushing moms is a showcase of the social contrasts that animate the neighborhood.

On the north side of the park, serving as a gateway to Fifth Avenue, is the **Washington Arch ❷**, built in wood in 1892 to commemorate the centennial of George Washington's presidential inauguration and later replaced by this marble version. **North Square ❸**, at the corner of Waverly Place, in the Washington Square Hotel, is a good choice for lunch.

Thankfully, NYU has spared the fine townhouses on Washington Square North, which are about the only 19th-century buildings still facing the park, apart from **Judson Memorial Church** on the opposite side. The church was designed in Romanesque Revival style by architect Stanford White in the early 1890s and is associated these days with a broad range of progressive issues and events, including a series of theatrical performances, gay lectures, and art exhibits.

Washington Mews

Walk about half a block up Fifth Avenue to **Washington Mews ❸** (gates closed

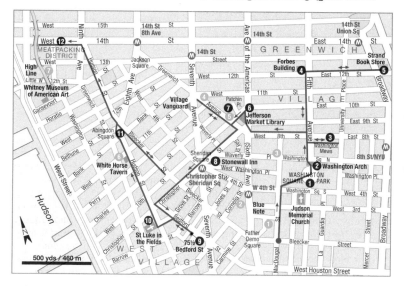

In Jefferson Market Library's community garden

at night), a cobbled alley that runs between Fifth and University Place. The pretty little row houses here were originally built as stables for the townhouses on Washington Square North and were later converted to artist studios.

A few blocks north along Fifth Avenue is the **Forbes Building** ❹, previously home to the handsome collection of art and vintage toys of Malcolm Forbes, the flamboyant late publisher of *Forbes*

magazine. Book-lovers should visit the **Strand Book Store** ❺ (three blocks east on 12th Street and Broadway; www.strandbooks.com; daily 9.30am–10.30pm; rare book room closes at 8pm), a New York institution. Italian author Umberto Eco describes this as his 'favorite place in America.' The owners claim to stock over two million volumes – from half-price review copies to $100,000 rarities. In 2017, the Strand celebrated its 90th birthday.

The nearby **Salmagundi Club**, at 47 Fifth Avenue, is the country's oldest artists' club, founded in 1870. Its facilities are for members only, but there are walk-in classes (www.salmagundi.org) should you fancy joining the artistic fraternity for a few hours.

Additionally, the Village is home to some of the world's most famous jazz clubs. First among equals is the **Blue Note** (131 West 3rd Street; www.bluenotejazz.com), which presents time-honored greats as well as contemporary acts. Also in the neighborhood, the **Village Vanguard** (178 Seventh Avenue South; www.villagevanguard.com) cut its teeth by launching jazz royalty like Miles Davis and John Coltrane. In 2015 it celebrated its 80th birthday.

WEST VILLAGE

Back on Fifth Avenue, head west on 8th Street, then north on Sixth Avenue for about a block to the **Jefferson Market Library** ❻, a Gothic confec-

The Whitney Museum

Housed in an impressive steel and concrete building designed by Renzo Piano, the Whitney Museum of American Art (99 Gansevoort Street; www.whitney.org; Wed–Mon 10.30am–6pm, Fri–Sat until 10pm; free daily tours) was relocated here from the Upper East Side in 2015. The Whitney collection was founded in 1931 by Gertrude Vanderbilt Whitney, whose tastes were for American Realists like Edward Hopper and George Bellows. Since then the museum's policy has been to acquire pieces that represent the full range of 20th-century American art, with works by Georgia O'Keeffe, Willem de Kooning, Jackson Pollock, and Jasper Johns. Every other year it mounts the Whitney Biennial (the next one is scheduled for spring–fall 2019), a survey of provocative new American art. Head to the Studio Café on the eighth floor for sweeping views across the Hudson River.

Strand Book Store   *MacDougal Street*

tion. Built as a courthouse in 1877 and later attached to a women's prison, this Victorian landmark is now a branch of the New York Public Library. Inmates included activist Angela Davis, Catholic reformer Dorothy Day, and accused spy Ethel Rosenberg. The prison was demolished in the 1970s, and a community garden stands in its place.

Loop around the library to West 10th Street, to find tiny **Patchin Place** ❼, whose residents included playwright Eugene O'Neill, journalist John Reed, and poet e. e. cummings.

Greenwich Avenue

If time permits, take a detour up **Greenwich Avenue**, which has numerous shops and restaurants. If you're in the mood for a bite, **Elephant & Castle** ❹, is found at No. 68, and **Rosemary's** ❺ at the corner of West 10th Street.

Christopher Street

Double back on Greenwich Avenue and turn right at **Christopher Street**. This is the traditional center of New York's gay community. Although much of the scene has now shifted north of 14th Street, it's still worth having a stroll around. Between Waverly Place and Seventh Avenue is the **Stonewall Inn** ❽ (53 Christopher Street; www.thestonewallinnnyc.com), site of a 1969 riot touched off by gay patrons fed up with being rousted by the police. The event is widely seen as the opening salvo in the gay rights movement. (The original bar was actually next door.)

Just across the street, tiny fenced-in **Christopher Park** has a statue of Civil War general Philip Sheridan. Sheridan Square itself isn't a square at all, it's actually at the triangular junction where Grove, Christopher, and West 4th streets meet.

Bedford Street

Follow Christopher across Seventh Avenue South, then turn left at Bedford Street into one of the quiet residential areas that make the Village such a pleasant place to live. The poet Edna St Vincent Millay lived at **75 ½ Bedford Street** ❾, said to be Manhattan's narrowest house at just over 9ft (3 meters) wide.

Hudson Street

Retrace your steps on Bedford Street, turn left at Grove Street, and continue one block to Hudson Street. Facing the intersection is the blocky, austere mass of **St Luke in the Fields** ❿, (www.stlukeinthefields.org) the city's third-oldest church, built in 1822.

Farther up Hudson Street, amid a cluster of boutiques, antique shops, and restaurants, is the **White Horse Tavern** ❻, a favorite of Welsh poet Dylan Thomas before he collapsed here in 1953 after one too many whiskeys. Thomas later died at nearby St Vincent's Hospital.

Bleecker Street

Beyond 11th Street, Hudson Street converges with a six-way intersection around

Alfresco dining in the hip Meatpacking District

cute and leafy **Abingdon Square ⑪**. This route concludes by heading northwest up Hudson Street to the Meatpacking District, where there are some great options for eating. Before making your way there, you could make a detour by turning right on **Bleecker Street**, where you can stroll around the antique shops and boutiques that line the street all the way to Sixth Avenue.

The early 2000s saw a boom in high-end fashion retailers along Bleecker Street, with the likes of Marc Jacobs and Ralph Lauren opening up several stores. Astronomic rents and disappointing footfall, though, meant it wasn't to last, and many of those stores now sit empty.

Bleecker is crossed by some of Greenwich Village's prettiest side streets. Bank Street is particularly lovely, with its cobblestones and pastel houses, as is Perry Street, which is one block farther along.

MEATPACKING DISTRICT

Northwest of Abingdon Square, the Meatpacking District was formerly a neighborhood of meat wholesalers and commercial butchers that has now become one of the city's most fashionable areas.

During the day, you can visit the **Whitney Museum of American Art** (see box) and browse high-end designers; there are a number on **West 14th Street ⑫** between Ninth and Tenth avenues: **Jeffrey New York** (No. 449), and Diane von Furstenberg (at the corner of Washington Street). If you're in need of a break, there's a clutch of restaurants around the cobbled intersection of Hudson, Gansevoort, and Little West 12th streets where you can stop for dinner or drinks.

It's a fairly laidback scene, and very different from the glitz of the nighttime hours, when thin, rich, and famous celebrities jam the restaurants and nightclubs, flashbulbs pop, and the hoi polloi gawk from behind velvet ropes.

The High Line

At the edge of the Meatpacking District, the High Line (www.thehighline. org) runs from Gansevoort to 34th Street between 10th and 11th avenues. This is a defunct, elevated freight railroad transformed into New York's most unusual park. Built in the early 1930s to serve upper-floor loading docks of factories and warehouses, the railroad delivered its last trainload of frozen turkeys in 1980 and was left to molder for 20 years, sprouting a natural garden of wildflowers and weeds. Seeing the potential, a group of friends successfully enlisted the city to save the tracks. The original wild plantings inspired the naturalistic landscaping along a concrete walkway that incorporates parts of the rails and the original metal fencing. It offers seating, and city and Hudson River views from a 30ft (9-meter) -high perspective. It extends as far as the Jacob Javits Center.

Just below the High Line on Washington Street, the **Standard Grill ⑦**, has good food and a great terrace.

Strolling along the High Line

Food and drink

● CAFFE REGGIO

119 MacDougal Street (between Bleecker and West 3rd streets); tel: 212-475-9557; www.cafereggio.com; daily B, L, and D; $
Beat poets Allen Ginsberg and Jack Kerouac once hung out here; today you're more likely to find NYU students, but it's still a cozy place to enjoy pastries, panini, pasta, and soups.

● PEARL OYSTER BAR

18 Cornelia Street (between Bleecker and West 4th streets); tel: 212-691-8211; www. pearloysterbar.com; Mon–Fri L and D; $$$
New York City's original oyster bar brought New England's celebrated seafood to Manhattan – think lobster rolls, clam chowder, and of course oysters.

● NORTH SQUARE

103 Waverly Place (at McDougal Street); tel: 212-254-1200; www.northsquareny. com; Mon–Fri B, L, and D, Sat–Sun B, Br, and D; $$
A relaxing oasis downstairs in the Washington Square Hotel serving good New American food at keen prices. Good lunch menu with prix-fixe option.

● ELEPHANT & CASTLE

68 Greenwich Avenue (between Perry and Seventh Avenue); tel: 212-243-1400; http://elephantandcastle.com; Mon–Fri B, L, and D, Sat–Sun Br and D; $

Tiny, sociable old-timer serving sandwiches, salads, burgers, and pub fare, plus a fine Sunday brunch. Try the dessert crepes.

● ROSEMARY'S

18 Greenwich Avenue (near 10th Street); tel: 212-647-1818; www.rosemarysnyc.com; Mon–Fri B, L, and D, Sat–Sun Br and D; $$
This enoteca and trattoria boasts a true rooftop garden, where they actually grow some of their ingredients, and is a bright and lively place for small bites and Italian classics.

● WHITE HORSE TAVERN

567 Hudson Street (at West 11th Street); tel: 212-989-3956; www.whitehorsetavern1880. com; daily L and D; $$
No bar tour of Greenwich Village is complete without visiting this historic watering hole, a favorite of students and assorted literati ever since Welsh poet Dylan Thomas, following his own advice, pulled up a barstool and went most ungently into that good night.

● STANDARD GRILL

Standard Hotel, 848 Washington Street (at 13th Street); tel: 212-645-4100; www. thestandardgrill.com; daily B, L, and D, Sat–Sun Br and D; $$
A unique location below the High Line and an excellent chef serving up American favorites make for a popular addition to the neighborhood. The outdoor terrace is a fine place for a drink at the end of the day.

Bargain goods in Canal Street

SOHO AND TRIBECA

*These neighborhoods are the very epitome of post-industrial chic.
They are urban playgrounds known the world over for cast-iron
architecture, stylish boutiques, loft living, and fantastic food.*

DISTANCE: 2.25 miles (3.5km)
TIME: A half- to full day
START: West Broadway
END: Tribeca Film Center
POINTS TO NOTE: The nearest subway stations to the starting point are Prince Street or Spring Street A, C, E. You may wish to build in some time during the tour for shopping in Soho. The tour ends at Tribeca, a great area for dining.

The old industrial neighborhood of Soho (**So**uth of **Ho**uston Street) was invaded by artists in the 1960s and soon after blossomed into a mecca of avant-garde culture. The artists, however, were soon priced out and most of the galleries have moved on, many of them to Chelsea. Today's neighborhood is devoted far more to shopping than to art.

This tour leads you through a few hot spots, though any number of distractions might lure you off the track. Soho's streets are narrow and the crowds can be daunting, especially on weekends, when many New York-

ers like to brunch and browse, so don't expect to zip through.

WEST BROADWAY

Start your tour at **West Broadway** ❶ near Houston Street. West Broadway is Soho's main drag and is lined with high-end boutiques including American giants **Oliver Peoples** (No. 366), **Ralph Lauren** (No. 381), and **Eileen Fisher** (No. 395), as well as European designer brands **French Connection** (No. 435) and **La Perla** (No. 434).

PRINCE STREET

The shopping district spills over into the cross streets, especially **Prince Street** ❷, which hosts **Marc Jacobs Crew** (No. 113), **Miu Miu** (No. 100), **Shinola** (No. 101), **Coach** (No. 143), and others.

While you're browsing, take a moment to admire two fine buildings at Prince and Greene streets: **112 Prince Street,** which on its eastern face has an extraordinary *trompe l'œil* mural by artist Richard Haas, and, on the opposite corner, **109 Prince**

Hanging on a Soho stoop

Street, a handsome five-story edifice with a cast-iron facade that houses a Polo Ralph Lauren men's boutique.

In a former post office a little farther on is the stylish **Apple Store** (103 Prince Street). Fight your way through the mob to try the latest iPads, iPhones, and other new gadgets. Farther along, at the corner of Mercer Street, is the **Mercer Hotel** (147 Mercer Street; see page 111), a trendy boutique hotel in a beautiful Romanesque Revival building. **Fanelli Café** ① is a good nearby eatery to stop at.

GREENE STREET

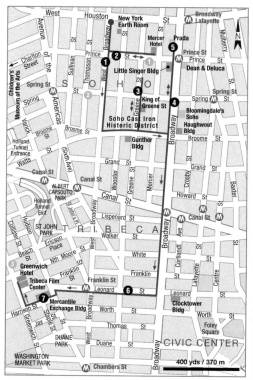

Retrace your steps to West Broadway and turn left. Browse the shops down to Broome Street, detouring after one block, right down Spring Street, for hot food at **Bistro Les Amis** ②, if sustenance is required. Turn left at Broome and continue to **Greene Street** ③. In the late 19th century, this was the center of a notorious red-light district, where brothels conducted business behind shuttered windows. Now the same windows attract a different sort of browser – those who gaze longingly at the latest designs by **Saint Laurent** (No. 80) and **Paul Smith** (No. 142).

Soho Historic Cast Iron District

Greene Street is also the heart of the **Soho Historic Cast Iron District**. Most of the structures here were constructed

in the mid- to late 1800s, when manufacturers moved into the neighborhood and needed to create industrial spaces quickly. There was no electricity, of course, so it was necessary for windows to admit a maximum of light. With rear walls often facing gloomy alleys, the only place sunlight could enter was through voluminous front windows. The solution to problems over expense came in the form of buildings with pre-cast iron facades that could be assembled on site. And since casting iron requires less labor than sculpting stone, the facades could be quite ornate.

The prominent **Gunther Building** at the corner of Greene and Broome streets is especially noteworthy. It was built in 1872 as a showroom and warehouse for fur dealer William Gunther and now serves as a collection of loft apartments.

BROADWAY

Take your time exploring Greene Street before returning to Broome Street and walking one block east to **Broadway ❹**. Pause here for a look at the landmark **Haughwout Building** (488–492 Broadway), a palazzo with five stories of arched windows, fluted columns, and prominent cornices, all rendered in cast iron. Built in 1857 for china dealer Eder V. Haughwout, the building was the first to install the newfangled 'safety elevator' invented by Elisha Otis, a development that opened the way for the

skyscrapers that would eventually dominate Manhattan's skyline.

Bloomingdale's and around
Despite the presence of a handful of tony stores, Broadway tends to appeal to shoppers with more mainstream tastes than West Broadway. Even smart **Bloomingdale's** (504 Broadway, near Broome Street; www.bloomingdales.com) caters to young, mid-market customers.

A few steps away is the landmark **Little Singer Building** (561 Broadway), a 12-story confection of terracotta, steel, and wrought-iron tracery built in 1904.

Brightly painted windows mark the entrance to the **Children's Museum of the Arts** (103 Charlton Street, near Greenwich Street; http://cmany.org; Mon–Fri noon–5pm, Thu until 6pm, Sat–Sun 10am–5pm), a space that is part museum, part art studio. Here children learn by becoming artists and everything is built half-size.

Across the street, gourmet shop **Dean & Deluca** (560 Broadway; www.deandeluca.com) lures foodies from throughout the city. The stand-up coffee bar is a good place for a snack, although the line of caffeine-starved New Yorkers can be fairly long.

Across Prince Street, in a building once occupied by a branch of the Guggenheim Museum, is fashion temple **Prada ❺** (575 Broadway), which has redesigned the interior in the shape of a half-pipe connecting the first and sec-

Shooting pool in a Tribeca bar

ond floors. It's worth a look inside even if you can't afford the merchandise.

TRIBECA

Head back down Broadway for 10 blocks until you reach Leonard Street. In the late 1970s, artists in search of lower rents migrated south from Soho to **Tribeca** (the **Tri**angle **Be**low **Ca**nal). An eclectic blend of renovated warehouses, Corinthian columns, condo towers, and narrow streets, Tribeca's attractions can easily be covered in a morning, leaving lots of time to do what Tribeca does best – indulge in eating. Some of Manhattan's best (and most expensive) bars and restaurants are here, but savvy visitors can soak up the atmosphere at a fraction of the cost by sampling a meal at lunch.

Leonard Street
Some of Tribeca's finest architecture is on **Leonard Street** ❻. Just to the east, the **Clocktower Building** (No. 108) is the former New York Life Insurance Building, remodeled by Stanford White in 1898.

Hudson and Harrison
Leonard ends at Hudson Street. On the corner of Hudson and Harrison is the ornate, recently restored **Mercantile Exchange Building** ❼, built in 1884 as the trading center for the egg and butter business. **Wichcraft**, see ❸, is on the corner of Beach and Greenwich.

Walk half a block west on Harrison, then two blocks north on Greenwich to the **Tribeca Film Center**, (www.tribeca-filmcenter.com) the offices of actor Robert De Niro and the hub of the Tribeca Film Festival. Although the center is closed to visitors, you can try your hand at power lunching in the **Tribeca Grill** (see page 120).

Food and drink

❶ FANELLI CAFE
94 Prince Street (at Mercer Street); tel: 212-226-9412; daily L and D; $
This holdover from Soho's industrial past still has the homey vibe of a neighborhood tavern. The kitchen knocks out a great burger.

❷ BISTRO LES AMIS
180 Spring Street (at Thompson Street); tel: 212-226-8645; www.bistrolesamis. com; daily L and D; $$
All the bistro classics plus pastas and salads are served at this friendly longtime neighborhood favorite.

❸ WICHCRAFT
397 Greenwich Street (at Beach Street); tel: 212-780-0577; www.wichcraft.com; daily B and L, early D; $
This handy mini-chain by star chef Tom Colichio (Craft) serves up gourmet sandwiches and paninis, plus a breakfast sandwich all day.

Cakes at Veniero's Pasticceria

EAST VILLAGE AND LOWER EAST SIDE

Take a stroll around St Mark's Place in the East Village, go shopping for new fashions in NoLita, check out the delis and boutiques of the Lower East Side, and take a tour of the Tenement Museum.

DISTANCE: 2.5 miles (4km)
TIME: A half-day
START: St Mark's-in-the-Bowery
END: Orchard Street
POINTS TO NOTE: The best day to do the route is Sunday, when the Orchard Street Market takes place. Whichever day you choose, be sure to book well in advance for the Tenement Museum.

This part of Manhattan is a series of neighborhoods that overlap and bump up next to each other in a convivial and vibrant way. What these areas have shared historically, aside from proximity, is a high-spirited funkiness. Gentrification is changing the mood, however. Today, these neighborhoods boast a growing number of top restaurants and boutiques that appeal to the young and hip. If you wish to fortify yourself with coffee and cake before exploring, try **Veniero's Pasticceria**, see ❶, a short walk from the starting point on East 11th Street.

EAST VILLAGE

The route starts in the **East Village**, which, even after years of gentrification, still has a bit of raw bohemian quality. In the late 1960s, this was the epicenter of East Coast counterculture, where Andy Warhol presented Velvet Underground 'happenings' and the scene at nightclubs like the infamous Electric Circus were heavily seasoned with psychedelic lights and hallucinogens.

But the East Village is much older than this. The church of **St Mark's-in-the-Bowery** ❶ (http://stmarksbowery.org), where this route begins, was built in 1799 on land that belonged to Peter Stuyvesant, the last Dutch governor of New York. Stuyvesant is buried in a nearby cemetery.

Cooper Square

At the end of Stuyvesant Street you will emerge onto **Cooper Square**. Ahead is an immense brownstone structure, **Cooper Union** ❷, established by inventor and entrepreneur Peter Cooper in 1859 as a college for the underprivileged. Abraham Lincoln made his famous 'Might Makes

Astor Place
Salamis at Katz's Delicatessen

Right' speech here in 1860, cementing his bid for the presidential nomination. The high-rise **Standard** hotel (www.standardhotels.com) is a very tangible sign of gentrification.

St Mark's Place

Turn around and head along the East Village's 'main street,' **St Mark's Place ❸**. The attitude here is a good-natured mix of punk, funk, and radical politics. Sidewalk cafés heave with customers, and the bazaar-like atmosphere is augmented by street vendors. Bars and restaurants are plentiful and filled with local characters.

Just by Tompkins Square Park is **Alphabet City**, so named because of its avenues A, B, C, and D. Once known for crime and poverty, many of its slums have been replaced by restaurants and bars that attract a hip young crowd. The **Museum of Reclaimed Urban Space** (155 Avenue C; www.morusnyc.org; Tue and Thu–Sun 11am–7pm), a block east of Tompkins Square Park, offers an interesting insight into how the local community has changed its neighborhood for the better, as well as offering walking tours of Alphabet City.

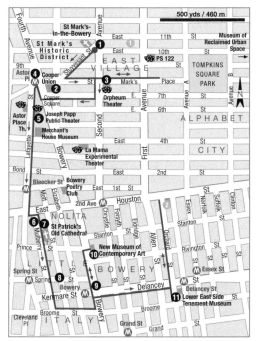

Public Theater

From McSorley's turn right and cross Cooper Square. A few steps north on Fourth Avenue is **Astor Place ❹**, where there is a handsome cast-iron subway kiosk, as well as a black cube by Tony Rosenthal called *The Alamo*.

Walk south on Lafayette Street to the **Public Theater ❺** (www.publictheater.org), headquartered in the majestic Astor Library, and built in the late 19th century. The theater is devoted to both

Buzzy Little Italy streets

Shakespeare and new plays, some of which have become major hits, like *Hair* and *A Chorus Line*.

NOLITA AND LITTLE ITALY

Continue four blocks south on Lafayette to East Houston Street. The area just south of Houston is a fun, savvy, boutique-laden lair known as **NoLita**. **Mulberry Street 6** is the heart of this temple to trendy retail, and there are lots of watering holes and restaurants in the surrounding side streets.

St Patrick's Old Cathedral 7 (http://oldcathedral.org) was the seat of the Catholic archdiocese until 1879, when the 'new' St Patrick's Cathedral on Fifth Avenue was completed. Services were held in Italian, highlighting the fact that this part of the city was in **Little Italy 8**.

Although NoLita (**No**rth of **L**ittle **Ita**ly) and **Chinatown** farther south have both encroached upon its borders, Little Italy is still an atmospheric place for a meal, especially during the Feast of San Gennaro, the annual 10-day event which is held during September. Head further down Mulberry Street to sample the atmosphere and the restaurants.

LOWER EAST SIDE

The Lower East Side, which slants south of East Houston Street to the East River, is where Jewish immigrants from Eastern Europe settled toward the end of the 19th century. In and around the early 20th century, this was the most densely populated place in the world, with as many as 1,000 people per acre on its mean streets.

These days you'll see Chinese or Hispanic stores that, despite retaining Jewish names, demonstrate that the neighborhood still attracts new arrivals. Lately these have included trendy young New Yorkers, and with them, the advent of the fashionable boutiques, bars, and hotels that thrive around Orchard, Ludlow, and Rivington streets.

Traditional eats

No tour of the Lower East Side is complete without visiting a few of the neighborhood's delis, bakeries, and candy shops. Tank up for a long day of walking at Yonah Schimmel Bakery (137 East Houston Street; www.knishery.com), where knishes – mounds of dough stuffed with potato, spinach, or kasha – are baked in a brick oven. A few doors away, you can pick up paper-thin lox (smoked salmon), caviar, and herring at Russ & Daughters (179 E. Houston Street; www.russanddaughters.com). Around the corner, Economy Candy (108 Rivington Street; www.economycandy.com) has been satisfying New York's sweet tooth since the 1930s. If you're near the Tenement Museum, try ice cream at Il Laboratorio del Gelato (188 Ludlow Street; www.laboratoriodelgelato.com) or a salty, garlicky pickle at The Pickle Guys (357 Grand Street; www.pickleguys.com).

In the Lower East Side Tenement Museum

The Bowery

East of NoLita and Little Italy is the **Bowery ⑨**, a long north–south street that gave this section of the Lower East Side its name. For years considered Manhattan's Skid Row, even this notoriously seedy strip is getting the Soho treatment, as posh nightclubs, designer shops, and million-dollar lofts open amid former flophouses and whiskey joints.

Underscoring this gentrification is the **New Museum of Contemporary Art ⑩** (No. 235 Bowery at Prince Street; www.newmuseum.org; Tue–Sun 11am–6pm, Thu until 9pm) showing avant-garde work by living artists.

Tenement Museum

From the art museum head south two blocks and turn left onto Delancey Street. Five blocks along is Orchard Street where, on the corner at No. 108, you will find the visitor centre for the **Lower East Side Tenement Museum ⑪** (www.tenement.org; Fri–Wed 10am–6.30pm, Thu until 8.30pm; tours daily). The museum is a thematic tour of an actual 1863 tenement building at No. 97. Over a span of seven decades this one building housed more than 7,000 people from some 20 countries. The building can only be seen by guided tour; these book up in advance and times vary, so call ahead or check the website for reservations. A limited number of same-day tickets are available at the visitor center.

Orchard Street to Houston

The best way to get further acquainted with this neighborhood is to walk up Orchard Street from the museum to Houston Street. If possible, visit on Sunday, when Orchard is at its busiest (many stores are closed Friday afternoon and Saturday in observance of the Jewish Sabbath).

Once crowded with peddlers selling cut-rate clothing, **Orchard Street** today still offers some discount designer fashions, but the old shops are giving way to quirky boutiques. There are also several cool cafés in the neighborhood, including the legendary **Katz's Delicatessen ②**.

Food and drink

① VENIERO'S PASTICCERIA

342 East 11th Street (near First Avenue); tel: 212-674-7070; www.venierospastry. com; Sun–Thu 8am–midnight, Fri–Sat 8am–1am; $
A classic Italian pastry shop and café founded in 1894.

② KATZ'S DELICATESSEN

205 East Houston Street (at Ludlow Street); tel: 212-254-2246; www.katzsdelicatessen. com; daily B, L, and D; $$
This Jewish deli is a New York institution, and the huge space is often filled to capacity. You might recognize it from the famous fake orgasm scene in the film *When Harry Met Sally*.

New York's skyline from the river

LOWER MANHATTAN

A tour of the Financial District, taking in the New York Stock Exchange, Federal Hall, Trinity Church, the 9/11 Memorial, and Battery Park, plus a walk along the Hudson River and a visit to the enduring South Street Seaport.

DISTANCE: 2.45 miles (4km)
TIME: A full day
START: Stock Exchange
END: South Street Seaport
POINTS TO NOTE: While this route could easily take a full day, you may wish to do the first half in the morning, including lunch at the World Financial Center, and then catch a ferry from Battery Park in the afternoon either to the Statue of Liberty and Ellis Island, or to Staten Island (route 16).

Lower Manhattan is the original New York, where winding streets lead to busy, international docks. Today, these narrow byways are lined by towering temples of finance, museums, elegant churches, and, on the eastern side, South Street Seaport, a complex of historic waterfront buildings, ships, dining, and shops.

Start this tour in the heart of the Financial District: outside the imposing neoclassical temple that houses the **New York Stock Exchange** ❶

on Broad Street just a few steps from Wall Street. Inside, the trading floor is a frenzy of buying and selling that, for better or worse, underpins the American economy.

WALL STREET

Walk to the corner of Wall Street and turn right for **Federal Hall** ❷ (26 Wall Street; www.nps.gov/feha; Mon–Fri 9am–5pm, some Sat in summer), a Greek Revival edifice built in 1842 on what was the site of the British City Hall. George Washington was inaugurated as the country's first president here in 1789. Inside are free exhibits focusing on American history with an emphasis on the role of New York City and its many prominent residents.

Just next door to Federal Hall is **40 Wall Street**, ❸ yet another New York skyscraper which once held the mantle of the world's tallest building (for a couple of months in 1930). Today this neo-Gothic masterpiece is part of Donald Trump's portfolio, hence its alternative name: the Trump Building.

A famous address

Trinity Church

Trinity Church

Double back on Wall Street about three blocks to Broadway, where the Gothic bell tower of **Trinity Church ❹** rises up like an exclamation point. Surrounding the church are some of the city's oldest graves. Just north of Fulton street, sits **St Paul's Chapel ❺** (209 Broadway), the city's oldest church, built in 1766. More modest than Trinity Church, St Paul's reflects the earlier Georgian style, and it too has a peaceful graveyard.

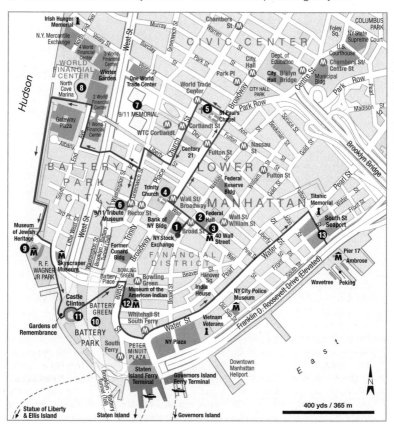

9/11 TRIBUTE MUSEUM AND WORLD TRADE CENTER SITE

The church borders Vesey Street on the northern end. Follow Vesey one block west and turn left onto Church Street, passing under the shadow of the 1,776ft (541-meter) -tall **One World Center**. Now the tallest building in the western hemisphere, it offers breathtaking views over the city from the One World Observatory deck on the 102nd floor (https://oneworldobservatory.com; daily 9am–8pm; until midnight in summer) and the ONE Dine restaurant on the floor below.

Back on the ground level, turn right on Liberty Street then left down Greenwich Street for a visit to the **9/11 Tribute Museum** ❻ (92 Greenwich Street; www.911tributemuseum.org; Mon–Sat 10am–6pm, Sun 10am–5pm). This non-profit organization was set up in the aftermath of the September 11, 2001 tragedy as a memorial to the tragedy, told through the stories of survivors and the family members of those who lost their lives. A documentary on life before the attack has testimonies from former employees and local residents, while other galleries focus on events as they unfolded, and the rescue and clean-up operation.

Turn back on yourself and walk north up Greenwich Street for three blocks, where you will reach the entrance to the **9/11 Memorial** ❼ (Greenwich and Albany streets; www.911memorial.org; daily 7.30am–9pm). The outdoor memorial is appropriately tranquil and somber;

entry is free, and guests are allowed to explore at their own pace so that everyone has sufficient time to pay tribute to the victims of the country's worst terrorist attack. White oaks surround the deep reflective waterfalls and pools that sit in the footprints of the two fallen towers. Names of the nearly 3,000 who died are etched into the walls of the pool. The accompanying museum (Sun–Thu 9am–8pm, last entry at 6pm; Fri–Sat until 9pm, last entry at 7pm) includes multi-media and interactive exhibitions that put the tragedy into historical context, while the cavernous Foundation Hall houses the last surviving column and retaining wall. Tickets are required for entry into the museum (www.911memorial.org).

WORLD FINANCIAL CENTER

Exit at the corner of Albany and West streets and head toward the Hudson River. Turn right on South End Avenue and follow it to the Brookfield Place, originally known as **World Financial Center** ❽. Here, a few shops and restaurants are clustered around the **Winter Garden**, a marble plaza with palm trees under a vaulted glass roof. If you're lucky, you might catch a lunchtime concert. Otherwise, take the opportunity to eat barbecue at **Blue Smoke** ❶.

HUDSON RIVER ESPLANADE

It's about a 10-minute walk south along the river **Esplanade** to the

A space for reflection at the 9/11 Memorial

Museum of Jewish Heritage 9 (36 Battery Place; www.mjhnyc.org; Sun–Fri 10am–6pm, Wed–Thu until 8pm, Fri until 5pm). The museum lies by the spot where Jews first set foot in North America in 1654. Exhibits draw from a rich pool of personal artifacts to present the story of the Jewish people and put the Holocaust into the context of 20th-century history.

Battery Park

Follow Battery Place to **Battery Park 10** at Manhattan's southern tip. Encompassed within its 21 acres (8 hectares) are gardens, walkways, and monuments.

At the water's edge is **Castle Clinton 11**, a stone fort built as a defense against the British during the run-up to the War of 1812 and later used as a theater, immigration station, and aquarium. It now serves as the ticket office for the **Statue of Liberty and Ellis Island ferries** (see page 96).

Bowling Green

Across State Street from Battery Park is the **National Museum of the American Indian 12** (1 Bowling Green, www.nmai.si.edu; daily 10am–5pm, Thu until 8pm), housed in the ornate Beaux Arts Custom House designed by Cass Gilbert in the early 1900s. The museum showcases highlights from a vast collection of Native American art held by the Smithsonian Institution.

The museum fronts a cobbled plaza known as **Bowling Green**, New York's old-est public park and site of the massive 7,000lb (3,000kg) bronze **Charging Bull**, created in 1989 by Arturo Di Modica. It is commonly believed among stockbrokers that rubbing a certain part of the bull's anatomy brings good luck to the market.

SOUTH STREET SEAPORT

From Bowling Green, State Street loops around past Whitehall Street and the **Staten Island Ferry Terminal** to Water Street, where you can either hail a cab, hop on a bus, or walk about 10 blocks to Fulton Street, then right to the **South Street Seaport 13** (12–14 Fulton Street; http://www.seaportdistrict.nyc). In the mid-1800s this was the country's busiest port, but the advent of large steamships shifted sea traffic to the deeper waters of the Hudson River. Flooding from Hurricane Sandy damaged many of the piers, galleries, and businesses here and the port underwent significant renovations, the last of which finished in summer 2018.

Food and drink

🍴 BLUE SMOKE

255 Vesey Street; tel: 212-889-2005; www.bluesmoke.com; daily L and D; $$

An upscale entry in New York's constantly evolving barbecue scene and a popular lunch spot for traders. It's a good choice for a quick, tasty and filling sit-down meal.

Lady Liberty

STATUE OF LIBERTY AND ELLIS ISLAND

Stop for coffee and pastries near Wall Street, then board the ferry to the monumental statue and historic building that received more than 12 million new arrivals during the great age of American immigration.

DISTANCE: 3 miles (5km)
TIME: A half-day
START: Stone Street
END: Battery Park
POINTS TO NOTE: Ferries to the Statue of Liberty and Ellis Island depart from Battery Park in Lower Manhattan every thirty minutes from approximately 8.30am to 3pm (seasonal variations). Tickets can be bought at Castle Clinton or online at www.statuecruises.com (tel: 877-523-9849 for more information). Free park-ranger-led tours of both islands are conducted daily. To climb to the Statue of Liberty crown, a pass is required; these are available at www.statuecruises.com.

This route's first port of call is **Financier Patisserie** ❶, on **Stone Street**, for coffee and pastries to set you up for the day. Once sated, head south to **Battery Park** ❶, for the ferry to the Statue of Liberty.

STATUE OF LIBERTY

The **Statue of Liberty** ❷ (Liberty Island; www.nps.gov/stli; ferries daily approx. 8.30am–3pm), or to give her full name, *Liberty Enlightening the World*, was a gift from the people of France, and was conceived by Edouard-René Lefebvre de Laboulaye, a Gallic admirer of American democracy.

De Laboulaye conveyed his enthusiasm to sculptor Frédéric-Auguste Bartholdi, who not only designed the monument but took a leading role in raising funds for its construction. The engineer Gustave Eiffel, who would later gain enduring renown for his eponymous tower erected for the 1889 World Fair, designed the trusswork that supports the copper skin.

The statue was completed in France in July 1884, and arrived in New York Harbor in June 1885 on board the French frigate *Isère*. In transit, Lady Liberty and her crown, torch, tablet, and other accessories were reduced to 350 pieces and packed in 214 crates. It took four months to reassemble the statue in its entirety. On October 28 1886, a dedication by President Grover Cleveland took place in front of thousands of spectators.

Faces of immigration at Ellis Island

ELLIS ISLAND

After visiting the statue, the ferry traditionally continues to **Ellis Island ❸**, which was for 62 years, from 1892 to 1954, the gateway to the United States, and known as the 'Island of Tears,' because of the stress caused to applicants by the strict medical, mental, and literacy tests imposed. Today, more than 100 million Americans are descendants of the around 12 million immigrants who landed at Ellis Island in search of a better life.

Immigration Museum

Allowed to fall into ruin after it was closed in 1954, the main building on the island was restored with $156 million in private funds, and in 1990 reopened as a museum. The **Ellis Island National Museum of Immigration** (www.ellisisland.org; ferries as for Statue of Liberty) chronicles the island's history through exhibits, photographs, artifacts, personal papers, and interactive displays that recreate the process of entering the country. A 45-minute audio tour, included with your ferry ticket, allows visitors to relive the immigrant experience.

After your tour of at least the statue, take time to enjoy the views of the Manhattan skyline, before catching a ferry back to the mainland.

STATEN ISLAND FERRY

The **Staten Island Ferry ❹** may be the best tourist deal in New York. The free, 20-minute ferry shuttles passengers between the Whitehall Terminal adjacent to Battery Park and St George Terminal on Staten Island. Views of the Statue of Liberty and Lower Manhattan are excellent. The panorama is especially inspiring after dark.

Food and drink

❶ FINANCIER PATISSERIE

62 Stone Street (at Mill Lane); tel: 212-344-5600; www.financierpastries.com; Mon–Sat B and L; $

Start the day with coffee and a choice of tarts, croissants, and other pastries at this delightful café on a cobbled side street closed to traffic. Lunch is nice, too, with soups, salads, and hot-press sandwiches. Outdoor tables shaded with umbrellas give the patisserie an authentic Parisian feel.

The Brooklyn Bridge looms large

BROOKLYN

Catch a subway train to the suburbs and unwind with the Brooklynites in Prospect Park, which is home to Brooklyn Botanic Garden and the wonderfully eclectic Brooklyn Museum of Art.

DISTANCE: 1.5 miles (2.5km)
TIME: A half- to full day
START/END: Grand Army Plaza
POINTS TO NOTE: This route focuses on the Prospect Park area of Brooklyn. To get to the starting point take the 2 or 3 train to Grand Army Plaza. If you want to spend longer in Brooklyn, consider a walk across the Brooklyn Bridge and/ or a visit to one of the borough's many neighborhoods, such as Brooklyn Heights or DUMBO.

Brooklyn is the city's most populated borough, connected to Lower Manhattan by the striking **Brooklyn Bridge**. Opened in 1883, it was called the 'eighth wonder of the world.'

Brooklyn has many neighborhoods, some dating from the borough's days of Dutch occupancy in the 1600s. One area that is always desirable is **Brooklyn Heights**; the Brooklyn Heights Promenade has handsome townhouses on one side and views of Manhattan and the East River on the other.

When Soho became too expensive, artists moved over the water to lofts in **DUMBO** (Down Under the Manhattan Bridge Overpass), then to Williamsburg and Red Hook. Any of these areas are worth an afternoon's visit, strolling around the galleries and shops.

PROSPECT PARK

Start at **Grand Army Plaza ❶**, a monumental square with a triumphal arch that serves as the entrance to 585-acre (237-hectare) **Prospect Park**. The park was designed in 1866 by Frederick Law Olmsted and Calvert Vaux and is thought by many to exceed their achievement in Central Park, which they designed eight years earlier. A short walk leads into **Long Meadow ❷**, a mile of gently sloping grassland where Brooklynites come to picnic, play ball, and generally unwind.

BOTANIC GARDEN

Return to Grand Army Plaza and a short walk east on Eastern Parkway leads to the

Grand Army Plaza

Cherry blossom at Brooklyn Botanical Gardens

Brooklyn Botanic Garden ❸ (www.bbg.org; Dec–Feb Tue–Sun 10am–4.30pm, Mar–Oct Tue–Fri 8am–6pm, Sat–Sun 10am–6pm, Nov Tue–Fri 8am–4.30pm, Sat–Sun 10am–4.30pm), which is made up of 52 acres (21 hectares) of specialty gardens, with a program of concerts and festivals.

BROOKLYN MUSEUM

Also accessible from Eastern Parkway is the **Brooklyn Museum** ❹

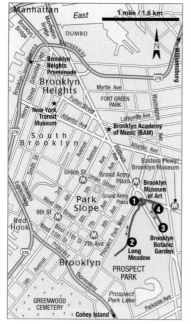

(www.brooklynmuseum.org; Wed–Sun 11am–6pm, Thu until 10pm), second only to the Metropolitan as New York City's largest art museum. There are 28 period rooms and an unusual outdoor sculpture garden. Scholars and art fans from all over the world come here to study the museum's respected Egyptian collection. Every first Saturday of the month, Brooklyn Museum extends its opening hours until 11pm. With free admission, music and dance shows in the lobby, and wine served in the late-closing Museum Café, there's quite a buzz.

For refreshment, try the aforementioned café, or the main restaurant, The Norm, helmed by Michelin-starred chef Saul Bolton. There are also some great alternative dinner and brunch options nearby, such as **Rose Water** ❶. Return to Grand Army Plaza and take Union Street three blocks northwest.

Food and drink

❶ ROSE WATER

787 Union Street; tel: 718-783-3800; www.rosewaterrestaurant.com; Mon–Fri D, Sat–Sun Br and D; $$$

With a dinky dining room and sheltered terrace, Rose Water does seasonal American food, with the focus on quality organic ingredients. The weekend prix-fixe brunch menu of eggs, waffles, and French toast is popular with locals.

In New York City Botanical Garden

THE BRONX

Take a day trip to the Bronx for a stroll through one of the world's premier botanical centers, a tour of the country's largest urban zoo, and dinner in New York's 'other' Little Italy.

DISTANCE: 3 miles (5km)
TIME: A half- to full day
START: Botanical Garden Station
END: Fordham Road Station
POINTS TO NOTE: Take the Metro–North Harlem local line from Grand Central Terminal to Botanical Garden Station. The journey takes 20 minutes (see www.mta.info). To return to Grand Central from Arthur Avenue, walk to Fordham Road Station (417 East Fordham Road at Third Avenue). The garden is closed Mondays and selected zoo attractions are closed in winter when some animals hibernate.

Food and drink

① DOMINICK'S

2335 Arthur Avenue (at 187th Street); tel: 718-733-2807; daily L and D; $$
Fans claim that this is the real Little Italy. There's no menu – the waiter tells you all you need – and no check: they just size you up and name a figure. Cash only.

In 1641 a Scandinavian, Jonas Bronck, bought 500 acres (200 hectares) of virgin forest from Native Americans. The Indian land was called Keskeskeck, but was soon known as 'Bronck's Land.' Part of the original hemlock forest remains in Bronx Park, which includes the two attractions covered here.

BOTANICAL GARDEN

From the Botanical Garden station walk across Kazimiroff Boulevard to the Mosholu Gate of the **New York Botanical Garden** ❶ (www.nybg.org; Apr–Dec Tue–Sun 10am–6pm, Jan–Mar Tue–Sun 10am–5pm). There are more than 40 specialty gardens, especially attractive in spring. The **Enid A. Haupt Conservatory** is a highlight, a crystal palace with a Palm Court and greenhouses constructed in 1902. The **Rockefeller Rose Garden** is a vision not to be missed in late May–early June, and the **Everett Children's Adventure Garden** has pint-size topiaries and mazes that make for hours of fun for youngsters.

Gorilla at Bronx Zoo   *Head to Arthur Avenue for an Italian meal*

BRONX ZOO

Next stop is the **Bronx Zoo ❷** (Bronx River Parkway and Fordham Road; www.bronxzoo.com; Apr–early Nov Mon–Fri 10am–5pm, Sat–Sun 10am–5.30pm, Nov–Mar daily 10am–4.30pm; free on Wed), a 20-minute walk away. To get here, exit the Botanical Garden from Conservatory Gate, turn left down Kazimiroff Boulevard, cross Fordham Road and continue along Southern Boulevard until you reach the pedestrian entrance on your left.

This is the largest metropolitan zoo in the US and home to around 4,500 animals, including endangered species. The attractions include a monorail ride over Wild Asia, a 40-acre (16-hectare) complex with moats to keep the big cats away from their prey (ie the spectators), and the Congo Gorilla Forest, 6.5 acres (2.5 hectares) of forest and bamboo thickets that are home to around 20 lowland gorillas. There's also a sea-lion pool, bison range, and children's zoo, as well as indoor facilities for nocturnal animals, reptiles, monkeys, and more.

LITTLE ITALY

Take a cab to end your tour with an Italian meal at **Dominick's ❶** in the **Belmont** neighborhood, the Bronx's Little Italy, around **Arthur Avenue ❸** and East 187th Street.

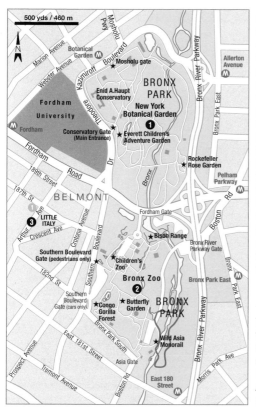

DIRECTORY

Hand-picked hotels and restaurants to suit all budgets and tastes, organised by area, plus select nightlife listings, an alphabetical listing of practical information, and an overview of the best books and films to give you a flavor of the city.

Room at Casablanca Hotel

ACCOMMODATIONS

New York hotels are the most expensive in the US and you may not get much space for your money, but some recent additions have made the city a bit more affordable. The five-star properties are as luxurious as any in the world, although tabs beginning at $600 a day will be beyond many travelers. The listings below feature a wider range of choices. Rates vary by season, with the low periods in winter and in August, but hotel websites may have special rates and packages at anytime. Many hotels offer discounts for longer stays or reservations booked well in advance. Discount websites are useful as well; www. booking.com has many New York offerings; www.kayak.com lets you compare several services on one site. Added to your hotel bill will be city, state, and occupancy taxes of 14.75 percent plus a room charge of $3.50 per night.

Students and other budget travelers might consider staying at one of several hostels. Most offer dorm-style lodging, shared bathrooms, and a common kitchen for a fraction of the cost of a standard hotel. Manhattan locations include Jazz

> Price for a double room for one night without breakfast:
> $$$$ = over $350
> $$$ = $250–$350
> $$ = $200–$250
> $ = under $200

on Columbus Circle (940 Eighth Avenue; tel: 646-876-9292); Chelsea International Hostel (251 West 20th Street; tel: 212-647-0010; www.chelseahostel.com); and HI-New York (891 Amsterdam Avenue; tel: 212-932-2300; http://hinewyork.org). Or of course, there's always the trusty YMCA (five locations; tel: 212-630-9600; www.ymcanyc.org/guest-rooms).

Bed and breakfast accommodations in New York range from a room in someone's apartment to a full apartment or small inn. For information, contact City Lights (tel: 212-737-7049; www.citylightsnewyork.com) or Bed and Breakfast Network of New York (www.bedandbreakfastnetwork.com/new-york). Or, of course, there's always Airbnb (www.airbnb.com).

Midtown

414 Hotel

414 West 46th Street (between Ninth and Tenth avenues); tel: 212-399-0006; www.414hotel.com; subway: 42nd Street Eighth Avenue; $$

Two brownstones with a courtyard between have been transformed into a best-bet budget boutique with a location perfect for Broadway theaters.

The Benjamin

125 East 50th Street (at Lexington Avenue); tel: 212-715-2500/866-222-2365; www.thebenjamin.com; subway: 51st Street; $$$

One of New York City's boutique-style

hotels, the Benjamin offers business and leisure travelers four-star amenities and some of the most comfortable beds in New York, at relatively reasonable prices. Rooms have galley kitchens with a microwave and fridge, and some have terraces. There is also a spa, fitness center, restaurant, and cocktail lounge. The lovely Art Deco building was erected in 1927, the work of world-renowned architect Emery Roth.

Casablanca Hotel

147 West 43rd Street (6th Avenue and Broadway); tel: 212-869-1212; www.casablancahotel.com; subway: Times Square 42nd Street; $$$

Wonderful small hotels are rare in New York, yet here is a lovely and inviting choice. The decor throughout evokes Morocco, with Murano glass hallway sconces and beautifully tiled and appointed bathrooms. Continental breakfast included.

Dylan Hotel

52 East 41st Street (at Madison Avenue); tel: 212-338-0500; www.dylanhotelnyc.com; subway: Grand Central 42nd Street; $$

A small, sleek, upscale boutique hotel at reasonable prices, centrally located blocks away from Grand Central Terminal. Housed in a 1911 Beaux Arts building once home to a chemists' society.

Hotel Edison

228 West 47th Street (at Broadway); tel: 212-840-5000; www.edisonhotelnyc.com; subway: 49th Street; $$$

Darkly stylish rooms are offered at reasonable prices in this 1931 hotel, whose lights were originally turned on by Edison himself. Though the Art Deco lobby can be chaotic, the rooms in this huge hotel are quite comfortable, pleasantly if simply decorated, and quiet. One of the best deals this close to Times Square.

The Hotel @ Fifth Avenue

17 West 32nd Street (near Fifth Avenue); tel: 212-736-1600/800-567-7720; www.applecorehotels.com; subway: 34th Street Herald Square; $$$

Like others in the Apple Core Hotels group, rates at this 182-room hotel, a short walk from Macy's and Madison Square Garden, are extremely reasonable, especially considering that the comfortable rooms come with free Wi-Fi and continental breakfast. There's also a 24-hour fitness center, an on-site gift shop, and an open-air rooftop bar where music and snacks can be enjoyed throughout the summer, along with views of the Empire State Building.

The Iroquois New York

49 West 44th Street (5th and 6th avenues); tel: 212-840-3080; www.iroquoisny.com; subway: Times Square 42nd Street; $$$$

This luxurious boutique hotel is close enough to the theater district to be convenient but far enough away to be out of the path of most of the crowds. Standard rooms are not large, but they accommo-

The library at Hotel Metro

date a king-size bed without feeling too cramped. The health club is first-rate.

The London NYC

151 West 54th Street (between Sixth and Seventh avenues); tel: 855-668-0072; www.thelondonnyc.com; subway: Seventh Avenue; $$$

The all-suite London boasts style and unusually large quarters for New York, not to mention a sleek bar-restaurant serving superb American cuisine throughout the day.

Lotte New York Palace

455 Madison Avenue (at 50th Street); tel: 800-804-7035; www.lottenypalace.com; subway: 5th Avenue 53rd Street; $$$

A grandiose monument to lavish pomp and excess and appointed in a style that can only be called postmodern Rococo, the Palace has a regime of flawlessly detailed service to make the average guest feel like an imperial pasha.

The Maxwell

541 Lexington Avenue (near East 49th Street); tel: 212-755-1200; www.maxwellhotelnyc.com; subway: 51st Street 6; $$$

This new hotel boasts stylish contemporary rooms with modern artworks and funky purple up-lighting, and several achingly stylish bars and restaurants including the iconic Whiskey Blue.

Hotel Metro

45 West 35th Street (between Fifth and Sixth avenues); tel: 212-947-2500; www.hotelmetronyc.com; subway: 34th Street Herald Square; $$

Popular with the fashion industry, the Metro has an Art Deco feel, spacious rooms that are updated regularly, and nice features like a library, rooftop terrace, and free Continental breakfast.

Michelangelo Hotel

152 West 51st Street (just west of Seventh Avenue); tel: 212-765-1900; www.michelangelohotel.com; subway: 49th Street N or R, 50th Street 1; $$$

An oasis of calm and elegance just off Broadway, this hotel offers old-world ambience and comfortable rooms at comfortable rates.

The Paramount

235 West 46th Street (at Broadway and 8th Avenue); tel: 212-764-5500; www.nycparamount.com; subway: 49th Street; $$

A mix of retro and contemporary in the heart of Times Square. The rooms and public spaces pay homage to the theater design of the 1920s but through a modern and minimalist lens: amenities include extravagant 'entertainment suites,' access to the hotel's iPads and iMacs, and a classic theater district bar. Rooms are small but well equipped.

Peninsula New York

700 Fifth Ave (at 55th Street); tel: 212-903-3927; www.peninsula.com; subway: Fifth Avenue West 53rd Street; $$$$

One of the city's most lavish hotels, where richly appointed rooms go for about $850

The Plaza's Palm Court

In the Plaza's Fitzgerald Suite

(slightly less with corporate rates). The hotel's health club and spa are truly luxurious. It's also in a prime location on Fifth Avenue and has a wonderful rooftop bar.

The Plaza

Fifth Avenue (at 59th Street); tel: 212-759-3000; www.theplazany.com; subway: Fifth Avenue; $$$$

One of New York's grandest hotels, The Plaza recently underwent a renovation that restored its Edwardian-style splendor. Rooms are furnished with antiques and adorned with murals. The Oak Bar and the Rose Club are favorite pre- and post-theater spots.

Ritz-Carlton New York Central Park

50 Central Park South; tel: 212-308-9100; www.ritzcarlton.com; subway: Fifth Avenue–59th Street; $$$$

One of New York City's most iconic hotels, this 19th-century property looms elegantly on the southern edge of Central Park. Everything about it says quality and old-school glamour, from the marble-bedecked bathrooms to the quietly luxurious guestrooms.

St Regis

2 East 55th Street (at Fifth Avenue); tel: 212-753-4500; www.stregisnewyork.com; subway: Fifth Avenue 53rd Street; $$$$

A grand Edwardian wedding cake of a building, filigreed and charmingly muraled (by the likes of Maxfield Parrish). The St Regis is a magnet for somewhat older, moneyed guests who appreciate the ambience of a more regal age. The location is good; as is the legendary King Cole Bar.

Wellington Hotel

871 Seventh Avenue (at 55th Street); tel: 212-247-3900; www.wellingtonhotel.com; subway: 57th Street F; $$

The side-street entrance in a congested neighborhood is useful and the location is great for Central Park, Lincoln Center, and Carnegie Hall. A reliable standby with reasonable rates.

Chelsea to Gramercy Park

Ace Hotel

20 West 29th Street (at Broadway); tel: 212-679-2222; www.acehotel.com/newyork; subway: 28th Street R; $$$

The former Breslin Hotel boasts a hip clientele, a celebrated restaurant and stylish rooms. Too bad there isn't much to do in the surrounding neighborhood.

The Evelyn

7 East 27th Street (at 5th Avenue); tel: 212-545-8000; www.theevelyn.com; subway: 28th Street; $$

Located in a historic building dating from 1903, it is conveniently close to Greenwich Village, Times Square, Fifth Avenue, and Union Square which are within walking distance.

Gramercy Park Hotel

2 Lexington Avenue (at Gramercy Park); tel: 212-920-3300; www.gramercyparkhotel.com; subway: 23rd Street 6; $$$$

A Grand Suite at the St Regis

Once a faded relic from the Jazz Age, this property was brought back to life as a swank boutique hotel adorned with rich velvets, modern art, and chandeliers. The Rose and Jade bars are favorite celebrity hangouts.

Hampton Inn Manhattan-Chelsea

108 West 24th Street (at 6th Avenue); tel: 212-414-1000; http://hamptoninn3.hilton.com; subway: 23rd Street; $

Hi-tech decor sets the tone at this Chelsea spot situated at the doorstep of the gallery scene. Great location for shopping on nearby Sixth Avenue.

Inn at Irving Place

56 Irving Place (near East 18th Street); tel: 212-533-4600/800-685-1447; www.innatirving.com; subway: 23rd Street 6; $$$$

This pair of graceful townhouses have been transformed into a facsimile of a country inn, with a cozy fireplace-lit tea salon and 12 elegant rooms and suites featuring four-poster beds. There's a nice little tearoom on the lower level and an atmospheric bar, the Cibar Lounge.

The NoMad

1170 Broadway (at 28th Street); tel: 212-796-1500; www.thenomadhotel.com; subway: 28th Street Broadway; $$$

In the heart of the elegant NoMad (North of Madison Square Park) neighborhood, this hotel is housed in a stately Beaux Arts building and has luxurious guestrooms modeled on the Old World elegance of European hotels. The star of the show, though, is the food, courtesy of chef Daniel Humm whose outfit around the corner, Eleven Madison Park, was crowned the best restaurant in the world in 2017.

The Roger

131 Madison Avenue (at 31st Street); tel: 212-448-7000/888-448-7788; www.therogernewyork.com; subway: 33rd Street; $$$$

The Roger has exchanged its sleek, stark style for a warmer approach, using bold colors and natural wood. The lobby has a soaring atrium, while the bedrooms are home-away-from-home cozy, with lots of space, thick bathrobes, down comforters, and iPod docking stations. The penthouses have lovely balconies with views of the Empire State Building.

Upper West Side

Arthouse Hotel NYC

2178 Broadway (at 77th Street); tel: 800-509-7598; subway: 79th Street; $$

As the name suggests, this hip new hotel has an artsy décor which offsets its historic surroundings. It is within walking distance of the American Museum of Natural History and prime Upper West Side shopping.

Excelsior Hotel

45 West 81st Street; tel: 212-362-9200; www.excelsiorhotelny.com; subway: 81st Street–Museum of Natural History; $$

Overlooking Central Park and the Museum of Natural History, this elegant hotel is classic New York. Guestrooms

The Ace Hotel's lobby

and common areas are decked out in rich dark wood, and there's some of the city's best Latin American food – not to mention mojitos – at the sultry Calle Ocho restaurant.

Lucerne Hotel

201 West 79th Street (at Amsterdam Avenue); tel: 212-875-1000/800-492-8122; www.thelucernehotel.com; subway: 79th Street; $$$

A 1904 landmark building has become the gracious Lucerne, with European-inspired decor and many amenities. The hotel's Nice Matin restaurant is a favorite in the neighborhood.

Marrakech Hotel

2688 Broadway (at West 103rd Street); tel: 212-222-2954; www.marrakechhotelnyc.com; subway: 103 Street 1; $

Decked out in colorful Moroccan decor, this definitely remains a budget spot with very small rooms, but has upgraded with amenities including all private baths, flatscreen TV, and massage shower heads. There's a café, lounge, and a Starbucks just next door.

Upper East Side

The Carlyle

35 East 76th Street (at Madison Avenue); tel: 212-744-1600; www.thecarlyle.com; subway: 77th Street 6; $$$$

Posh, reserved, and serene, the Carlyle remains a highly acclaimed luxury hotel. The appointments are exquisite, the furnishings antique, the service formal. The hotel is the home of Café Carlyle and Bemelmans Bar, two of the city's most enduring upscale evening spots.

Courtyard by Marriott Upper East Side

410 East 92nd Street; tel: 212-410-6777; subway: 96th Street and Second Avenue; $$$

A comfortable, functional hotel with modern (if unremarkable) guestrooms with fast Wi-Fi, flat-screen TVs and a well-equipped fitness center among the amenities. There's no on-site dining, but no end of restaurants and cafés to choose from nearby.

The Franklin

164 East 87th Street (between Lexington and Third avenues); tel: 212-369-1000; www.franklinhotel.com; subway: 86th Street 4, 5, 6; $$$

This boutique hotel has upgraded and is not the bargain it once was, but look out for special rates. Despite very small rooms, the atmosphere is charming, the complimentary breakfast delicious, and the beds heavenly. Guests enjoy Wi-Fi access, nightly wine and cheese reception, and 24-hour coffee.

The Mark

Madison Avenue at 77th Street; tel: 212-744-4300/866-744-4300; www.themarkhotel.com; subway: 77th Street; $$$$

The Mark is a model of contemporary luxury, offering a range of rooms and suites at its prestigious Upper East Side address. Its acclaimed restaurant is the vision of celebrity chef Jean-Georges Von-

Bemelmans Bar at the Carlyle

gerichten. Special offers on the hotel website make it more affordable.

The Surrey

20 East 76th Street (at Madison and 5th avenues); tel: 212-288-3700/888-419-0052; www.thesurrey.com; subway: 77th Street; $$$$

This Beaux Arts gem's rooms are as elegant as any in this tony neighborhood, and the hotel is home to an impressive art collection. Grab a meal at the Café Boulud restaurant, just off the lobby; in the summer, check out the rooftop garden for a rare experience that is often exclusive to locals with penthouses.

Hotel Wales

1295 Madison Avenue (at 92nd Street); tel: 212-876-6000/866-925-3746; www.hotelwalesnyc.com; subway: 96th Street 6; $$$

The Wales offers a great location in Carnegie Hill, near Museum Mile and Central Park. Feast on the city's best breakfast next door at Sarabeth's East, or head to Paola's on the hotel's ground floor for superb Italian cuisine in a cozy trattoria setting, from fortifying brunches to hearty pasta dinners.

Greenwich Village and the Meatpacking District

Hotel Gansevoort

18 Ninth Avenue (at 13th Street); tel: 212-206-6700/877-426-7386; www.gansevoorthotelgroup.com; subway: Eighth Avenue; $$$$

The Meatpacking District's first luxury hotel has a rooftop bar and swimming pool, and breathtaking views. Bedrooms are fashionably appointed, if a little gaudy (if you don't like pink you may wish to look elsewhere). If your room faces west, the Hudson River will be on the horizon and the Meatpacking action will be taking place directly below, nonstop.

The Standard Hotel

848 Washington Street (at 13th Street); tel: 212-645-4646; www.standardhotels.com; subway: Eighth Avenue; $$$$

The High Line passes under the elevated Standard Hotel, where rooms are decked out with leather furniture, glass tables, and a fully modern sheen. In the winter, there's an ice rink. Year-round it has one of the Meatpacking District's most popular bars and restaurants, The Standard Grill.

Washington Square Hotel

103 Waverly Place (near Macdougal Street); tel: 212-777-9515; www.washingtonsquarehotel.com; subway: West Fourth Street; $

A century-old hotel that offers an ideal Village location on Washington Square Park. The rooms are small but nicely appointed. In a former incarnation, this was the seedy Hotel Earle, where Papa John Phillips of the 1960s folk group The Mamas & the Papas wrote the folk-rock classic *California Dreamin'*.

A light and airy suite at The Mark

Soho and Tribeca

Duane Street Hotel

130 Duane Street (near Church Street); tel: 212-964-4600, www.duanestreethotel.com; subway: Chamber Street; $$$

This small, sleek new contemporary hotel offers moderate rates in a pricey neighborhood.

Greenwich Hotel

377 Greenwich Street (near Moore Street); tel: 212-941-8900; www.thegreenwichhotel.com; subway: Franklin Street; $$$$

Robert De Niro and partners planned this exceptional luxury hotel with a residential feel. It offers a warm sitting room with fireplace and a landscaped courtyard, extra-spacious guest rooms, and an indoor pool. Rustic-elegant decor mixes Tibetan rugs, Moroccan and Italian tiles, old wood beams, and Asian antiques with paintings by De Niro's father.

Mercer Hotel

147 Mercer Street (near Prince Street); tel: 212-966-6060/888-918-6060; www.mercerhotel.com; subway: Prince Street; $$$$

This 1890s landmark has 75 rooms with high loft ceilings, Wi-Fi access, flat-screen televisions, and (for New York) spacious bathrooms. Andre Balazs, the owner, also owns Chateau Marmont in Los Angeles, and the clientele here is equally stylish and high profile. Facilities include a roof garden, a lobby bar with 24-hour food and drink service, complimentary gym access, and the highly regarded Mercer Kitchen restaurant and café.

SoHo Grand

310 W. Broadway (near Canal Street); tel: 212-965-3000; www.sohogrand.com; subway: Canal Street A, C, E; $$$$

Expect excellent service at this 15-story hotel, with industrial-chic decor and magnificent upper-floor views. Rooms have large windows. The lobby and bar are the rendezvous of choice for cool media types and rock stars.

Lower East Side

Hotel on Rivington

107 Rivington Street (near Ludlow Street); tel: 212-475-2600; www.hotelonrivington.com; subway: Delancey Street; $$$$

This sleek glass-walled hotel is bringing a dash of contemporary style to the gentrifying Lower East Side.

Lower Manhattan

Eurostars Wall Street

129 Front Street; tel: 212-742-0003; www.eurostarshotels.co.uk/eurostars-wall-street; subway: Wall Street 2, 3; $$

This sophisticated four-star has an understated feel, with generously sized, sleekly appointed rooms and a hearty American breakfast served each morning.

Holiday Inn Express Wall Street

126 Water Street (at Pine Street); tel: 212-747-9222/800-311-1216; www.ihg.com; subway: Wall Street 2, 3; $$

Business and pleasure meet here, with high-speed internet and work stations in every room as well as homey design touches.

Hip design at Blue Fin

RESTAURANTS

In a city with more than 20,000 restaurants, New Yorkers dine out a lot. With restaurants just steps from their doors there is no reason for them not to enjoy the best the city has to offer, and visitors should do the same. You'll find some of the best restaurants in the United States of America in New York, and some are quite expensive. But you won't have to take out a second mortgage on your home to eat well in this city – even in Manhattan. The variety of restaurants and eating options is unsurpassed. You can enjoy Indian dosas from a street vendor, dine at the newest celebrity chef's restaurant, or simply enjoy a really great meal at a favorite neighborhood spot.

Midtown

21 Club
21 W. 52nd Street (at 5th and 6th avenues); tel: 212-582-7200; www.21club.com; Mon–Fri L and D, Sat D only; subway: Fifth Avenue 53rd Street; $$$$

Price guide for a three-course dinner for one:
$$$$ = over $70
$$$ = $50–70
$$ = $25–50
$ = under $25

This ex-speakeasy will never be out of style with Manhattan's movers and shakers. Miniature jockeys line the exterior, while other corporate toys hang from the ceiling. A plaque over Table 30 reads 'Bogie's Corner.' Sip his favorite tipple, Ramos gin fizz, and order the chicken hash.

Becco
355 West 46th Street (between Eighth and Ninth avenues); tel: 212-397-7597; http://becco-nyc.com; daily L and D; subway: 49th Street N, R, W; $$
Lidia Bastianich's restaurant row mainstay offers three daily pasta preparations for less than $25 and bottles of wine for $33. One of the city's great deals.

Blue Fin
W Times Square Hotel, 1567 Broadway (between 46th and 47th streets); tel: 212-918-1400; www.bluefinnyc.com; daily B, L, and D; subway: 49th Street N, R, W; $$$
It's easy to be swept away by this seafood restaurant's over-the-top decor; in the street-level bar only a glass wall separates diners from the hubbub of Times Square. The sushi is sublime, and 'cooked' dishes such as sesame-crusted tuna and pan-roasted bass are a close second.

Brasserie Ruhlmann

45 Rockefeller Plaza (between Fifth and Sixth avenues); tel: 212-974-2020; www.brasserieruhlmann.com; Mon–Sat L and D, Sun Br; subway: 47–50 Streets – Rockefeller Center; $$$

A bit of 1920s Paris in Rockefeller Center. This inviting café was named for Art Deco designer Emile-Jacques Ruhlmann and pays homage with Deco decor. Chef Laurent Tourondel gets top marks for his bistro offerings. The shady patio invites lingering.

Bryant Park Grill

25 West 40th Street (at Sixth Avenue); tel: 212-840-6500; www.bryantparkgrillnyc.com; daily L and D, Sat–Sun also Br; subway: Fifth Avenue 7; $$$

A wall of glass and a generous terrace make the most of the park's leafy surroundings. The food almost lives up to the setting, with a menu of grilled and roasted fish and meats.

DB Bistro Moderne

55 West 44th Street (near Sixth Avenue); tel: 212-391-2400; www.dbbistro.com; daily B, L, and D; subway: 47–50 Streets – Rockefeller Center; $$$$

Offering modern gastronomy in a vintage setting, chef Daniel Boulud's bistro is awash with Art Deco glitz, well-heeled publishing types and trendy tourists. The foie gras and truffle burger is typical of the kitchen's culinary surprises.

Four Seasons

42 East 49th Street (at Madison Avenue); tel: 212-754-9494; www.fourseasonsrestaurant.com; Mon–Fri L and D, Sat D only; subway: Fifth Avenue/53rd Street; $$$$

Since it opened nearly 50 years ago, the Four Seasons has had a clientele to rival any *Who's Who* listing. In a new location, the decor remains timeless and the seasonal classics served are impeccable.

La Bonne Soupe

48 West 55th Street (between Fifth and Sixth avenues); tel: 212-586-7650; http://labonnesoupe.com; daily L and D; subway: 57th Street N, R, F; $$

When cash is low, head for this old-time French bistro, a safe bet since 1973 for crêpes, quiche, fondues, and great onion soup as well as *steak frites* and *poulet*. Reserve ahead or be prepared to stand in line.

La Grenouille

3 East 52nd Street (between Fifth and Madison avenues); tel: 212-752-1495; http://la-grenouille.com; Tue–Sat L and D; subway: Fifth Avenue/53rd Street; $$$$

One of the last great French eateries in Midtown, where a *quenelle* is still a *quenelle* and the flowers have rarely been more beautiful. A classic.

Oceana

120 W. 49th Street (at 6th and 7th avenues);

High-end dining at Jean-Georges

tel: 212-759-5941; www.oceanarestaurant. com; Mon–Fri B, L and D, Sat–Sun D; subway: 47–50 Streets – Rockefeller Center; $$$$

Spectacular seafood and one of the city's best raw bars served in the ground floor of the McGraw Hill Building. If tables aren't available, the 50ft (15-meter) marble bar is gorgeous and a good alternative.

Smith & Wollensky

797 Third Avenue (49th Street); tel: 212-753-1530; www.smithandwollenskynyc. com; Mon–Fri L and D, Sat–Sun only D; subway: 51st Street 6; $$$

This New York institution is usually packed with stockbrokers and Midtown executives, who come for the great steaks, extensive American wine list, and clubby, masculine atmosphere. The adjacent Wollensky's Grill is more casual and a bit less expensive.

Trattoria Dell'Arte

900 Seventh Avenue (at 56th Street); tel: 212-245-9800; www.trattoriadellarte.com; daily L and D; subway: 57th Street/Seventh Avenue; $$$

The fabulous antipasto bar doubles as a main course at this popular trattoria near Carnegie Hall. The seafood, pasta, and gourmet pizza are good choices, too.

Via Brasil

34 West 46th Street (between Fifth and Sixth Avenues); tel: 212-997-1158; www. viabrasilrestaurant.com; daily L and D; subway: 47–50 Streets – Rockefeller Center; $$

On the street known as 'Little Brazil,' this is a great place to try authentic specialties including big portions of beef *feijoada*, a stew that is the Brazilian national dish. There are chicken and fish dishes, too, if you don't favor red meat.

Upper West Side

Dizzy's Club Coca-Cola

33 West 60th Street (near Broadway); tel: 212-258-9595; www.jazz.org/dizzys; daily D; subway: 59th Street Columbus Circle; $$

The music and menu are red hot at Jazz at Lincoln Center's supper club, which dishes out Latin and Creole cuisine with a side of live jazz.

Gari

370 Columbus Avenue; tel: 212-362-4816; www.sushiofgari.com; Tue–Fri L and D; subway: 79th Street; $$$

One of an acclaimed local chain of upscale sushi restaurants, with classic Japanese dishes given a unique twist thanks to Masatoshi 'Gari' Sugio's signature range of sauces. Just behind the American Museum of Natural History.

Jean-Georges

Trump International Hotel, 1 Central Park West; tel: 212-299-3900; www.jean-georges.com; daily L and D; subway: 59th Street Columbus Circle;

A gourmet dessert at Daniel

Daniel's dining room

$$$

The skyscraper on chaotic Columbus Circle is an unlikely location for one of the city's most sophisticated and relaxing retreats. Chef Jean-Georges Vongerichten delights diners with creative versions of French classics. The bill can soar as high as the building, but the *prix-fixe* lunch at the adjoining Nougatine brings these gastronomic heights within reach. Book ahead.

Kefi

222 W. 79th Street; tel: 212-873-0205; http://michaelpsilakis.com; Mon–Fri L and D, Sat–Sun Br and D; subway: 79th Street B, C;
$$

One of the finest Greek restaurants in the city, where the crowd is always lively and the food is simultaneously comforting, traditional, and innovative.

Harlem

Amy Ruth's

113 West 116th Street (between Lenox and Seventh avenues); tel: 212-280-8779; www.amyruths.com; Tue–Sun B, L, and D, Mon L and D; subway: 116th Street; $

This restaurant attracts celebrities from the worlds of politics, sports, and entertainment, but the big pull is the classic Southern food.

Sylvia's

328 Malcolm X Boulevard (between 126th and 127th streets); tel: 212-996-0660; www.sylviasrestaurant.com; Mon–Sat B, L, and D, Sun Br and D; $$

'The queen of soul food,' Harlem's best-known eatery, serving hearty Southern dishes in large portions. It is always filled with tour groups so reserve ahead.

Upper East Side

Beyoglu

1431 Third Avenue (at 81st Street), 2nd floor; tel: 212-650-0850; daily L and D; subway: 77th Street 6; $$

Middle Eastern flavors burst from dishes such as yogurt rice soup, lamb kebab, hummus, and sauteed eggplant at this meze restaurant named after an Istanbul neighborhood. The portions are ideal for sharing, so come with a group and explore the whole menu.

Daniel

60 East 65th Street (near Park Avenue); tel: 212-288-0033; www.danielnyc.com; Mon–Sat D; subway: Lexington Avenue/63rd Street; $$$$

Master chef Daniel Boulud presides over this expensive food kingdom, but gourmands will gladly spend for the unique quality and service he delivers. The cuisine is mostly French with a few unexpected (but not gimmicky) twists, and the service is impeccable.

The Loeb Boathouse

Park Drive North; tel: 212-517-2233; www.thecentralparkboathouse.com; Apr–Nov daily D, Mon–Fri L, Sat–Sun Br; subway: 77th Street 6; $$$$

A great lakefront setting either in the airy, glass-fronted dining room or on the waterside terrace. Seafood is a specialty here, along with the pan-seared rack of lamb.

Mighty Quinn's BBQ

1492 2nd Avenue, Daily L and D; tel: 646-484-5691; www.mightyquinnsbbq.com; $

Hearty Southern soul food meets hipsterish design and a lively, youthful clientele at this popular barbecue joint, which has other branches across the city. The burnt end baked beans and brisket will linger long in the memory.

Chelsea to Gramercy Park

Cookshop

156 Tenth Avenue (at 20th Street); tel: 212-924-4440; Mon–Fri B, L, and D; Sat–Sun Br and D; www.cookshopny.com; subway: 23rd Street; $$

Support from local farmers means the freshest ingredients at this unpretentious Chelsea spot with good American food. Weekend brunches are wildly popular.

Empire Diner

210 Tenth Avenue; tel: 212-335-2277; www.empire-diner.com; Daily B, L, and D; subway: 23rd Street C, E; $$

This beloved Art Deco institution kickstarted the craze for upscale retro diners, and became beloved by celebrities including Steven Spielberg, Meryl Streep, and other such luminaries. It remains a buzzy, reliable spot for classic American diner dishes.

Friend of a Farmer

77 Irving Place (between 18th and 19th streets); tel: 212-477-2188; www.friendofafarmer.com; Mon–Fri B, L, and D, Sat–Sun Br and D; subway: Union Square; $$

It feels like a Vermont inn at this cozy restaurant serving hearty portions of American fare. Great for families.

Gramercy Tavern

42 East 20th Street (between Broadway and Park Avenue); tel: 212-477-0777; www.gramercytavern.com; daily L and D; subway: Union Square; $$$$

The Gramercy's New American cuisine is artfully prepared, and the handsome dining room has a homey feeling. Be sure to leave room for the chocolate pudding cake.

Novità

102 East 22nd Street (between Park and Lexington avenues); tel: 212-677-2222; www.novitanyc.com; Mon–Fri L and D, Sat–Sun D; subway: 23rd Street 6; $$$

This northern Italian restaurant remains an undiscovered gem. Expect delicious, freshly prepared dishes, gracious service, and reasonable prices.

Union Square Café

101 East 19th Street; tel: 212-243-4020;

www.unionsquarecafe.com; daily L and D, Sat–Sun Br; subway: Union Square; $$$$

A winning formula of top-flight food and service makes this a favorite of residents and tourists. The atmosphere is casual, but in a studied way. The chefs make full use of local ingredients sold by farmers at Union Square's Greenmarket to create a menu of mostly American fare, with a distinctly Italian accent.

Greenwich Village and the Meatpacking District

AOC

314 Bleecker Street (at Grove Street); tel: 212-675-9463; www.aocnyc.com; daily B, L, and D; subway: Christopher Street Sheridan Square; $$

The dishes are served here as simply and perfectly as in a Paris bistro. Unlike other hurried New York spots, here *le savoir-vivre* reigns, and you can linger and talk all night if no one needs your table. There's a little garden patio for summer, too.

Blue Hill

75 Washington Place (between Sixth Avenue and Washington Square West); tel: 212-539-1776; www.bluehillfarm.com; daily D; subway: West 4th Street; $$$$

A mellow, sophisticated spot that gets rave reviews for beautifully conceived American dishes made with fresh ingredients from the Blue Hill family farm.

Bubby's

73 Gansevoort Street; tel: 212-219-0666; www.bubbys.com; daily B, L and D, Sat–Sun Br; subway: 14th Street; $$

Few places are as inviting on a cold New York winter's day as this friendly diner, which specializes in hearty, simple comfort food done well – think fried chicken and pancakes, buttermilk biscuits and juicy steak sandwiches.

Buddakan

75 Ninth Avenue; tel: 212-989-6699; www.buddakannyc.com; daily D; subway: 14th Street; $$$$

A flamboyant, old world-European dining room, with Baroque chandeliers and wood-panelled walls, belies the pan-Asian menu at this upmarket restaurant. Tasting menus also available.

Camaje

85 MacDougal Street (between Bleecker and Houston streets); tel: 212-673-8184; http://camaje.com; daily D; subway: West 4th Street; $$

Chef Abigail Hitchcock prepares top-notch French bistro dishes with imagination and heart. Wednesdays and Saturdays see blindfolded 'dinner in the dark' events (tickets required). The casual atmosphere and reasonable prices make this a real find.

Charlie Bird

5 King Street; tel: 212-235-7133; www.

charliebirdnyc.com; Mon–Fri L and D, Sat Br and D, Sun Br only; subway: Houston Street; $$

Achingly hip New American joint, with an ethos inspired by the great creative minds of the city, with nods to Basquiat, Warhol, the Beastie Boys et al. The menu has an Italian slant, with a fantastic pasta selection.

Del Posto

85 Tenth Avenue (between 15th and 16th streets); tel: 212-497-8090; www.delposto.com; Mon–Fri L and D, Sat–Sun D; subway: 14th Street; $$$

Mario Batali's most ambitious showplace on the edge of the Meatpacking District lives up to its palazzo feel, with Italian food that reviewers have called 'heavenly.' Despite the formal setting, the staff is friendly and the piano music relaxing. The Italian wine list is enormous.

Fig & Olive

420 West 13th Street; tel: 212-924-1200; http://www.figandolive.com; daily L and D; subway: Christopher Street; $$

Thanks to chef April Bloomfield, this tiny, casual restaurant elevates pub food to gourmet status. Sit on plump cushions at small tables or perch on a stool and dig into chicken liver parfait, squid and mussel salad, or slow-braised beef shin with risotto. For a calmer scene, visit at lunch.

Pearl Oyster Bar

18 Cornelia Street (between Bleecker and West Fourth streets); tel: 212-691-8211; www.pearloysterbar.com; Mon–Fri L and D, Sat D; subway: West Fourth Street; $$

This raw bar is tucked into a side street populated by other small restaurants. Chowder is served, in addition to what some call 'perfection on the half-shell.'

Philip Marie

569 Hudson Street; tel: 212-242-6200; www.philipmarie.com; Tue–Sun Br, L and D; subway: Christopher Street; $$

New American doesn't have to equal pretentious, as this laid-back bistro proves. Superb, simple dishes, from New York steak to Baja fish tacos, are served in a cozy environment.

East Village, Little Italy, and Lower East Side

Caracas Arepa Bar

93½ E. 7th Street (at 1st Avenue and Avenue A); tel: 212-228-5062; www.caracasarepabar.com; daily L and D; subway: Astor Place; $

Locals flock to this casual Venezuelan restaurant for warm cornmeal pancakes topped with savory meat and vegetable options, served with hot sauce.

Indochine

430 Lafayette Street (at Astor Place and 4th Street); tel: 212-505-5111; www.indochinenyc.com; daily D; subway: Astor

Place; $$$

Trendy, tropical décor and French-Vietnamese food; this place is still sexy after all these years. It's located across from the Public Theater, and offers a decently priced pre-theater deal.

Momofuku Noodle Bar

171 First Avenue (between 10th and 11th streets); tel: 212-777-7773; https://momofukunoodlebar.com; daily L and D; subway: First Avenue; $$

The original outpost of the Momofuku empire, a hip place to get a bowl of ramen, some peerless pork buns, and a Korean-style fried chicken dinner for four. Also check out Momofuku Ssam Bar, Ko, and Milk Bar, all in the neighborhood.

Puglia

189 Hester Street (at Mulberry Street); tel: 212-966-6006; www.pugliaofnyc.com; daily L and D; subway: Canal Street J, N, Q, R, 6; $$

The Little Italy of old has persisted here since 1919. Things get 'pretty crazy' at night, according to the manager Joey, but group tables, a singer called 'The Fat Lady,' plus lots of red sauce and red wine make it a party every night.

Soho

Balthazar

80 Spring Street (near Crosby Street); tel: 212-965-1414; www.balthazarny.com; daily B and D, Mon–Fri L, Sat–Sun Br; subway: Spring Street; $$$

Parisian-style brasserie serving traditional bistro fare from breakfast until late. This spot is so popular, it's now hard to imagine Soho without it.

Blue Ribbon

97 Sullivan Street (at Spring Street); tel: 212-274-0404; www.blueribbonrestaurants.com; daily D; subway: Spring Street C, E; $$$

Popular for over 20 years, this Soho dining room and nightspot boasts an excellent raw bar and robust American classics. It's open late for bar crawlers, night owls, and chefs coming off their shifts.

The Butcher's Daughter

19 Kenmare Street (at Elizabeth Street); tel: 212-219-3434; www.thebutchersdaughter.com; B, L, & D daily, Sat–Sun Br; subway: Bowery; $$

With a hipster, industrial-chic design and a menu of hearty pastas and pizzas, zingy salads and grilled sandwiches, this buzzing vegetarian café creates exquisite plant-based eats.

Jane

100 West Houston Street (near Thompson Street); tel: 212-254-7000; http://janerestaurant.com; Mon–Fri L and D, Sat–Sun Br and D; subway: Houston Street or Spring Street;

Tribeca hotspot Odeon

$$

There's nothing plain about this Jane, where creative American dishes such as honey-braised pork and grilled sirloin are crafted from fresh, locally grown ingredients. Be sure to leave room for dessert.

Tribeca

Gunbae

67 Murray Street (at West Broadway); tel: 212-321-2500; www.gunbaetribeca.com; daily L and D; subway: Chambers Street; $$

Riding the wave of the Korean barbecue craze is this bustling restaurant, with exposed brick walls and seating along low wooden benches. Come for the wagyu brisket and kimchi hot pot, stay for the karaoke.

Little Park

85 West Broadway (at Chambers Street); tel: 212-220-4110; www.littlepark.com; daily B and D, Mon–Fri L, Sat–Sun Br; subway: Chambers Street 1, 2, 3; $$$$

If you're prepared to pay a little more for fresh, seasonal ingredients, try this upscale eatery in the Smyth Hotel. Farms from upstate provide organic chicken and beef, while big eye tuna and striped bass come courtesy of the coast.

Locanda Verde

377 Greenwich Street (at North Moore Street); tel: 212-925-3797; www.locandaverdenyc.com; daily B, Br, L, and D; subway: Franklin Street; $$$

Expertly treading the line between hip and haute, this wildly popular Italian restaurant showcases the best of rustic Italian cuisine and has become a Tribeca favorite.

Odeon

145 W. Broadway (at Duane and Thomas streets); tel: 212-233-0507; www.theodeonrestaurant.com; Mon–Fri L and D Sat–Sun Br and D; subway: Franklin Street; $$$

One of the first Tribeca hotspots, this Art Deco brasserie has been a mainstay ever since Warhol and Basquiat used to drop by. Come earlier in the day to avoid the crowds.

Tribeca Grill

375 Greenwich Street (at Crosby Street); tel: 212-941-3900; www.myriadrestaurantgroup.com; Mon–Fri L and D, Sat D only Sun Br; subway: Franklin Street; $$$

Co-owned by actor Robert De Niro and chef Drew Nieporent, customers flock here in the hope of seeing celebs from the Tribeca Film Center talking 'back story' and making deals.

Lower Manhattan

Delmonico's

56 Beaver Street (at William Street); tel: 212-509-1144; www.delmonicos.com; Mon–Fri L and D, Sat D; subway: Wall

Street 2, 3; $$$$
Wall Street deal-makers congregate at this clubby, chummy, old-time steakhouse. Beef is the specialty, of course, but the lobster, oysters Rockefeller, and other seafood dishes are quite good, too.

Gigino at Wagner Park

20 Battery Place (at West Street); tel: 212-528-2228; www.gigino-wagnerpark.com; daily L and D; subway: Bowling Green; $$
With sunset views of the Statue of Liberty, this moderately priced Italian could easily pander to tourists, but the food is high-quality and creative. When the weather is fine, the terrace is irresistible.

Harry's Café

1 Hanover Square (at Pearl and Stone streets); tel: 212-785-9200; www.harrysnyc.com; Mon–Sat L and D, Sun Br; subway: Wall Street 2, 3; $$
Folks refused to accept that the original Harry's closed, so the owners reopened it, offering great steaks and seafood.

Brooklyn

Talde

369 Seventh Avenue (at 11th Street); tel: 347-916-0031; www.taldebrooklyn. com; Tue–Sat D, Sat–Sun Br, D; subway: Seventh Avenue; $$
'Proudly inauthentic' is the tagline at this pan-Asian Brooklyn favorite, where chef Dale Talde throws away the rulebook to fuse flavors from India, Japan, the Philippines and beyond; try the crispy oyster and bacon pad Thai.

The Bronx

Roberto's

603 Crescent Avenue (at 186th Street); tel: 718-733-9503; www.robertosbronx. com; Mon–Sat L and D; train: Fordham; $$
Roberto will pop out of the kitchen in his whites to meet and greet, while his floury-handed mama may say hello in between preparing batches of pasta. A true slice of Italian life. When it's time to leave, catch a cab to Fordham Road station; you should take extra care in this neighborhood.

Performance at The Bowery Ballroom

NIGHTLIFE

The opportunities for entertainment and nightlife in New York could provide different diversions 365 days a year. Additionally, note that summer brings free Shakespeare, opera, and popular music concerts to Central Park. There is also free music and outdoor movies in many city parks.

Theater

Broadway

New York's Theater District is home to 40 active theaters, most on the side streets off Broadway, spanning Sixth to Eighth avenues between 41st and 53rd streets. For a list of current shows and theaters, see www.broadway.org.

Lincoln Center Theater

150 West 65th Street between Broadway and Amsterdam Avenue; tel: 212-239-6200; www.lct.org

The 1080-seat Vivian Beaumont and the 299-seat Newhouse, Lincoln Center stage both large-scale and intimate musical and dramatic plays.

Manhattan Theatre Club

Samuel Friedman Theater, 261 West 47th Street; tel: 212-239-6200; Stage 1, New York City Center, 131 West 55th Street; tel: 212-581-1212; www.manhattantheatreclub.com

Founded in 1970, this company produces many notable plays, including American premieres of works by playwrights such as Alan Ayckbourn.

Public Theater

425 Lafayette Street (between East 4th Street and Astor Place); tel: 212-539-8500; www.publictheater.org

Founded as the Shakespeare Workshop and still sponsors of free Shakespeare in the Park, the Public has grown into a showcase for the new and experimental. *Hair* and *A Chorus Line* were born here.

Roundabout Theatre Company

Tel: 212-719-1300; www.roundabouttheatre.org

The city's largest repertory company with 40,000 subscribers, four theaters, and countless awards, the Roundabout was founded in 1965 to revive classics. It later expanded to include new works.

Live music

Beacon Theatre

2124 Broadway; tel: 212-465-6000; www.msg.com/beacon-theatre

One of New York City's most legendary venues, the Beacon opened in 1929 as a vaudeville house and cinema, and is now one of the city's best and most beloved music venues. The elegant neoclassical Greek theater has hosted everyone from Bowie to Bob Dylan, and continues to welcome the great and the

Many special events are held at Carnegie Hall

good of music (and comedy) through its doors.

The Bitter End
147 Bleecker Street, between Thompson and Laguardia; tel: 212-673-7030; www.bitterend.com

A Greenwich Village landmark, the Bitter End books an eclectic mishmash of folk, folk rock, soft rock, blues, some comedy and cabaret... whatever. A classic example of eternal bohemianism, it's popular with tourists and can be mobbed on weekends.

Bowery Ballroom
6 Delancey Street (between Bowery and Christie streets); tel: 212-533-2111; www.boweryballroom.com

The 'in' spot to hear the best bands in concert, including top indie-rock bands.

Brooklyn Academy of Music
30 Lafayette Avenue, Brooklyn; tel: 718-636-4100; www.bam.org

Best known as BAM, the city's oldest performing arts center is also the most progressive, offering avant-garde companies in dance, music, opera, and theater. Easy to reach by subway from Manhattan.

Carnegie Hall
57th Street (at Seventh Avenue); tel: 212-247-7800; www.carnegiehall.org

Famed for its acoustics since its opening in 1891, this landmark concert hall seating 2,800 presents the world's top musicians and orchestras, from classical to jazz.

Lincoln Center
Broadway (between 63rd and 65th streets); schedules and tickets for all except Metropolitan Opera, tel: 212-721-6500; opera tickets, tel: 212-362-6000; www.lincolncenter.org

The city's cultural hub is home to the Metropolitan Opera House; the New York City Ballet at the David Koch Theater; the New York Philharmonic Orchestra at David Geffen Hall; the Chamber Music Society of Lincoln Center; and the Juilliard School of Music.

New York City Center
West 55th Street (between Sixth and Seventh avenues); tel: 212-581-1212; www.nycitycenter.org

This 1923 building was Manhattan's first performing arts center, and the 2,730-seat auditorium hosts dance companies like Paul Taylor and Alvin Ailey, as well as the much-loved Encores! series, revivals of vintage musicals.

Webster Hall
125 East 11th Street; tel: 212-353-1600; www.websterhall.com

Discount passes can be had by booking online for this large, always-jam-packed East Village club which attracts a young crowd. Open Wednesdays to Saturdays from 10pm, it offers all-night dance sessions for fans of everything from rock, reggae, and R&B to house, techno, and who

Village Vanguard

knows; theme nights range from 'runway parties' to 1960s psychedelia. Recently, it has been welcoming big-name rock and rap acts in its Grand Ballroom.

Jazz venues

Blue Note

131 West 3rd Street; tel: 212-475-8592; www.bluenotejazz.com

The West Village is home to the most famous jazz clubs in the world, and first and foremost is the Blue Note, packed virtually every night for years. The reason is simple: the club presents the very best of mainstream jazz and blues, from time-honored greats to more contemporary acts. The line-up has featured such luminaries as the Modern Jazz Quartet, Etta James, Joe Williams, Betty Carter, the Count Basie Orchestra... the list goes on and on. For diehard fans, there's a late-night session that jams until 4am, after the last set.

Iridium

1650 Broadway (at 51st Street); tel: 212-582-2121; www.theiridium.com

Relocated from the Upper West Side, this club/restaurant has presented some of jazz's most gifted denizens. Definitely worth checking out, especially Monday nights, when late guitar legend Les Paul's backing band is often holding court and hosting notable musicians like Marshall Crenshaw and Graham Parker.

Jazz at Lincoln Center

23 West 60th Street, Time Warner Center;

tel: 212-258-9800; www.jazz.org

This showcase for jazz high atop the Time Warner Center includes the 1,233-seat Rose Theater for concerts and the Jazz Hall of Fame. The Appel Room for cabaret and Dizzy's Club Coca-Cola, a jazz club, feature walls of glass framing city lights.

Smoke

2751 Broadway (between 105th and 106th streets); tel: 212-864-6662; www.smokejazz.com

Latin jazz, jazz, blues, and soul vocalists at this Uptown haunt; no cover charge for most late-night shows.

Village Vanguard

178 Seventh Ave South; tel: 212-255-4037; www.villagevanguard.com

Born over 70 years ago in a Greenwich Village basement, this flagship club cut its teeth helping to launch talents like Miles Davis and John Coltrane. In its adulthood, it hardly keeps up with the 'vanguard' anymore, but presents the greats and near-greats of what is now the mainstream. It's also a chance to catch acts that rarely tour. The VV is a terrific evening out, but an extremely popular one – call well in advance or book online to avoid disappointment.

Nightclubs

Baby's All Right

146 Broadway Brooklyn; tel: 718-599-5800; http://babysallright.com

This eatery, bar, and concert venue in hip Williamsburg offers excellent DJ sets

Drinking in the West Village

Slam poetry at Nuyorican Poets Café

and tasty food, and has swiftly become a local musical institution.

Bemelmans Bar

The Carlyle, 35 East 76th Street and Madison Avenue; tel: 212-744-1600; www. rosewoodhotels.com

Charming Bemelmans murals are the backdrop at this upscale gem offering the best in jazz combos, piano, and song.

Cielo

18 West Little 12th Street; tel: 212-645-5700; www.cieloclub.com

Meat Packing District clubs come and go, but Cielo seems to stay on top, with the best DJs and loyal fans packing the sunken dance floor.

Joe's Pub

425 Lafayette Street (at Astor Place), Public Theater; tel: 212-539-8500; http://joespub.publictheater.org

Cabaret, jazz, rock, poetry – eclectic shows are always excellent here, the atmosphere is intimate, and you can order drinks and dinner to enjoy during the show.

SOB's

204 Varick Street (between Hudson Street and Sixth Avenue); tel: 212-243-4940; www.sobs.com

Sounds of Brazil are only the start. Reggae to blues or hip hop might be on at this lively club, which also offers dinner and dancing.

Comedy and cabaret

Don't Tell Mama

343 West 46th Street; www. donttellmamanyc.com; tel: 212-757-0788

A merry spot, long favored by a theatrical crowd. In the front there's a piano bar; the back room is non-stop cabaret, with comedians and torch singers. Leave inhibitions behind, and bring cash (no credit cards accepted for cover and drink minimum).

Gotham Comedy Club

208 West 23rd Street; tel: 212-367-9000; www.gothamcomedyclub.com

The country's finest comedians, from Jerry Seinfeld to Jim Gaffigan, have cut their teeth at this Chelsea institution – and what's more, they keep coming back. Small-scale, combative and electric, this is classic New York comedy.

Nuyorican Poets Café

236 East 3rd Street (between Avenues B and C); tel: 212-780-9386; www.nuyorican.org

From poetry slams and hip-hop to multimedia, comedy, and music, at a cutting-edge East Village landmark.

Upright Citizens Brigade Theatre

207 West 26th Street; tel: 212-366-9176; www.ucbtheatre.com

Improv comedy at its most bizarre and inventive. This is where television stars like Amy Poehler and many cast members of *Saturday Night Live* got their start – they still take the stage from time to time.

On Fifth Avenue

A–Z

A

Airports and arrivals

New York's major international airports are John F. Kennedy and Newark Liberty International in nearby New Jersey. Allow an hour's driving time for each, more during rush hours. LaGuardia, serving domestic and Canadian flights only, is a 30-minute drive.

AirTrain is a subway-to-rail connection between JFK and the city (tel: 877-535-2478; www.airtrainjfk.com), or there are regular trains from Penn Station to Newark Airport (tel: 888-EWR-INFO; www.airtrainnewark.com). NYC Airporter (tel: 718-777-5111; www.nycairporter.com) operates buses to and from LaGuardia and JFK from the Port Authority Bus Terminal, Penn Station, Grand Central Terminal, and some Midtown hotels. Olympia Trails (tel: 877-8-NEWARK; www.CoachUSA.com/Olympia) runs express buses between Newark Airport and the Port Authority Bus Terminal, Penn Station, and Grand Central Terminal.

Door-to-door minibus service between Manhattan and all airports is provided by Super Shuttle (tel: 800-258-3826; www.supershuttle.com) and AirLink (tel: 212-812-9000; www.goairlinkshuttle.com). Prices are attractive, but allow an extra two hours for additional passenger pick-ups on the way.

Taxis to Midtown run $35–40 from LaGuardia, fixed price $52 from JFK, about $60 from Newark, plus tolls. Many travelers use private limo services such as Carmel (tel: 212-666-6666; www.carmellimo.com), with rates only slightly more than taxicabs.

C

Children

Preparation – and lots of patience – are the keys to a successful trip with children. In some respects, New York is the perfect family destination because there are so many activities that both adults and children will enjoy: a Broadway show, for example, or a trip to the Central Park Zoo. For kids who aren't accustomed to big-city life, even mundane experiences will be an adventure. You may be smitten by the city's art and culture, but what your kids may remember most is riding the subway, a playground or bike ride through Central Park, or buying hot dogs from a street vendor.

Climate and clothes

New York City has four distinct seasons (see page 11). Average

Harlem streets   *A classic New York building in Chinatown*

annual rainfall is 44in (112cm); rain-coats and umbrellas are a good idea year-round.

Dress tends to be casual, but it is advisable to ask about smarter dress for restaurants, nightclubs, etc.

Crime and safety

Despite its recent reputation as a 'caring, sharing New York,' parts of the city can hold hazards, and visitors should not be lulled into a false sense of security. Adopt the typical New Yorker's guise of looking street-smart and aware at all times and avoid ostentatious displays of jewelry or wealth that invite muggers. Excursions into deserted areas at night (such as Central Park or Battery Park) are equally unwise. Lock your hotel door even when you are inside, and travel to neighborhoods like Harlem in a group. Although Times Square has thrown off its seedy reputation, the crowded streets around this area attract pickpockets, so keep wallets in a secure place.

Although the subways are much safer than they were, people traveling alone late at night should stay on alert. Once through the turnstile, stay within sight of the ticket booth and try to get on a car where there are other people.

Customs regulations

For information on US Customs regulations, go to www.cbp.gov.

Disabled travelers

All city buses and a few major subway stops are accessible, as are most restaurants. Disabled travelers can obtain information about rights and special facilities from the Mayor's Office for People with Disabilities (tel: 311/212-NEW-YORK; www.nyc.gov/mopd).

Driving in New York

Driving is the least efficient way to get around. Drivers are aggressive, traffic is frequently snarled, street parking is scant (and tickets are punitive), and commercial parking is extremely expensive.

If a car is needed, rentals are available at airports and all over the city. You must be at least 21 to rent a car, have a valid driver's license, and a major credit card. Be sure you are insured for both collision and personal liability.

Dogs

If you're traveling with a dog, keep in mind that it must be leashed in public places, and droppings must be cleaned up and disposed of properly. Scoopers are sold at pet shops and hardware stores, but many dog owners find it easier to use a plastic bag.

Drinking age

The legal drinking age in New York is 21. Be prepared to show picture iden-

tification before purchasing alcohol or entering a bar. Some nightclubs admit under-21 patrons but card everyone who attempts to buy a drink.

E

Electricity

Standard American electric current is 120 volts. An adapter is necessary for European appliances, which run on 220–240 volts.

Embassies and consulates

Australian Consulate-General: 150 East 42nd Street; tel: 212-351-6500; http://newyork.consulate.gov.au.
British Consulate-General: 845 Third Avenue; tel: 212-745-0200; www.gov.uk/government/world/organisations/british-consulate-general-new-york.
Canadian Consulate-General: 466 Lexington Aveue; tel: 212-596-1628; https://international.gc.ca.
Consulate General of Ireland: 345 Park Avenue; tel: 212-319-2555; www.dfa.ie/irish-consulate/newyork.
New Zealand Mission to the UN: 600 Third Avenue; tel: 212-826-1960; www.mfat.govt.nz.
Consulate of South Africa: 333 East 38th Street; tel: 212-213-4880; www.southafrica-newyork.net.

Emergency numbers

Police, fire, ambulance: tel: 911.
Referral service: tel: 311.

Dental emergency: tel: 212-486-9458.
Health emergency: tel: 212-737-1212.
Report Sex Crimes: tel: 212-227-3000.

Entry regulations

Information on US entry regulations is found at travel.state.gov.

Etiquette

New Yorkers have a reputation for being brusque and outspoken. It's a generalization, but not entirely unfounded. This is a fast-paced city with a hard-charging attitude. That said, you will find that most citizens are very helpful if you seek assistance. This is also an extraordinarily diverse city. And while New Yorkers are hardly paragons of universal brotherhood, they manage to get along in a sort of workaday fashion that keeps the city from flying apart at the seams.

H

Health and medical care

Medical services are extremely expensive. Purchase comprehensive travel insurance to cover any emergencies.

A source if you need non-emergency house calls is Doctors on Call: tel: 718-238-2100.

Emergency medical treatment
Bellevue Hospital: 462 First Avenue

The departure hall at Grand Central Station

and East 27th Street; tel: 212-562-4141.

Mount Sinai Beth Israel Hospital: First Avenue at 16th St; tel: 212-420-2000.

Lenox Hill Hospital: 77th Street and Park Avenue; tel: 212-434-2000.

Mount Sinai Hospital: One Gustave L. Levy Place; tel: 212-241-6500.

New York Presbyterian Komansky Children's Hospital: 525 East 68th Street; tel: 212-746-5454.

New York Presbyterian Medical Center at Columbia University: 630 West 168th Street; tel: 212-305-2500.

NYU Langone Medical Center: 550 First Avenue at 33rd Street; tel: 212-263-7300.

Mount Sinai St Luke's Hospital: 1111 Amsterdam Ave; tel: 212-523-4000.

Hours and holidays

Business hours

Department stores and shops tend to stay open later, typically 10am to 8.30pm. Sunday hours are shorter, usually 11am to 6 or 7pm. Banks are normally open 9am to 3pm (although ATMs are everywhere), but increasingly they are opening as early as 8am and staying open until late afternoon or early evening.

Public holidays

The US has shifted most public holidays to the Monday closest to the actual dates, thereby creating a number of three-day weekends. Holidays that are observed no matter the day on which they fall are:

New Year's Day (January 1).
Independence Day (July 4).
Veterans' Day (November 11).
Christmas Day (December 25).
Other holidays are:
Martin Luther King Jr Day (third Mon in Jan).
President's Day (third Mon in Feb).
Memorial Day (last Mon in May).
Labor Day (first Mon in Sept).
Columbus Day (second Mon in Oct).
Election Day (first Tue in Nov).
Thanksgiving (fourth Thu in Nov).

Internet

Free public Wi-Fi is available in Union Square, Bryant Park, Chelsea Market, South Street Seaport, the Winter Garden (World Financial Center), Lincoln Center Park, public libraries throughout Manhattan, and in numerous cafés and restaurants. For the latest update check out www.wififreespot.com or www.nycgo.com/articles/wifi-in-nyc. Most hotels provide Wi-Fi (often at an additional fee) in their guest rooms, too. Email can be sent from most branches of FedEx Office shops or from computers at most public libraries.

LGBTQ travelers

The traditional epicenter of New

Consulting the map in Central Park

York's large gay community used to be Greenwich Village – the West Village in particular, on and around Christopher Street – but recently the center of gravity has shifted to Chelsea. Other popular neighborhoods are the East Village and Hell's Kitchen, in the 40s, west of the Theater District. Gay and lesbian travelers will find Manhattan a mostly tolerant and friendly place with a host of bars and clubs where gays congregate. Pride Week in late June is celebrated with a big Fifth Avenue parade, and the annual flamboyant Halloween Parade in Greenwich Village brings thousands of spectators.

Useful resources

Lesbian, Gay, Bisexual and Transgender Community Center: 208 West 13th Street (at Seventh Avenue); tel: 212-620-7310; www.gaycenter.org; Mon–Sat 9am–10pm, Sun 9am–9pm. This large and helpful organization offers services and events ranging from health education, counseling, and political action to parties.

Gay and Lesbian Hotline: tel: 212-989-0999; Mon–Fri 4pm–midnight, Sat noon–5pm. Provides information about all aspects of gay life in New York, from bars to legal counseling.

Gay & Lesbian Anti-Violence Project: 240 West 35th Street; tel: 212-714-1141; www.avp.org. Organization providing legal advocacy for victims of anti-gay violence.

Gay Men's Health Crisis: 307 West 38th Street; tel: 212-367-1000; www.gmhc.org. This non-profit group assists people with HIV/AIDS.

Newspapers and magazines

Gay City News: http://gaycitynews.nyc. Covers local, national, and world news.

Time Out New York Magazine: www.timeout.com/newyork. Runs a large weekly listing of gay clubs and events.

Lost property

The chances of retrieving lost property are not high, but the occasional civic-minded individual may turn items in to the nearest police precinct. To inquire about items left on public transportation go to http://lostfound.mtanyct.info (subway and bus), or call 511 or 311.

M

Maps

NYC & Co. has good maps at their visitor center and online at www.nycgo.com. Subway and bus maps are available at subway station booths, or from the New York City Transit Authority booth in Grand Central Terminal and the Long Island Rail Road information booth in Penn Station. You can also download them from new.mta.info.

Media

Print

The *New York Times* and *Wall Street*

Little Italy decorations

One–way street signs

Journal are both regarded as papers of national significance, and they are also strong on local issues. The *Times'* bulky Sunday edition has extensive coverage of local arts and entertainment.

Two papers compete for the tabloid market: the New York Post and the Daily News. There are two 'commuter' dailies distributed free in the mornings: AM New York and Metro. Local magazines with extensive event listings include New York and Time Out New York; Time Out is biweekly and can be picked up for free in many cafés and stores.

Radio

There are more than 70 radio stations in New York City. Some of the better stations with local news include:

WNYC: 93.9FM/820AM
WABC: 770AM
WCBS: 880AM
WINS: 1010AM
WBBR: 1130AM

Television

The three major networks – all with New York headquarters – are ABC (Channel 7, 77 West 66th Street; tel: 212-456-2700), CBS (Channel 2, 524 W. 57th Street; tel: 212-975-3525), and NBC (Channel 4, 30 Rockefeller Plaza; tel: 212-664-3700). Fox News has a national office at 1211 Sixth Avenue (tel: 212-301-3000) and a local studio (Channel 5, 205 East 67th Street; tel: 212-452-3983). CNN has offices at the Time Warner Center. Channel 13, the local Public Broadcasting Service (PBS) affiliate, has open studios at Lincoln Center. The other local stations are UPN (9) and CW (11).

Various cable companies offer hundreds of specialized cable and movie channels. Check newspaper listings for channel numbers.

With advance planning, it's possible to join the audience of a New York-based TV show, many of them shown overseas. Tickets are often free and sometimes distributed by lottery. For details, go to www.nycgo.com or see the website of your favorite program.

Money

Credit cards and ATMs

Cash advances on major credit and debit cards can be obtained from bank tellers and bank ATMs (automatic teller machines), which are marked with the corresponding stickers (ie Cirrus, Plus, Visa, MasterCard, American Express, etc.) Most of these charge a fee for withdrawing cash. Credit cards are accepted almost everywhere, although not all cards at all places.

Currency exchange

There are many outlets for exchanging currency and cashing travelers checks. These are accepted in many (but by no means all) hotels and restaurants (as

long as they are in dollars) and can be cashed at most banks. Some banks charge a fee for this service. Photo identification is required.

Travelex, a well-known source for currency exchange, has three convenient Midtown locations, tel: 516-300-1622; 1578 Broadway at 47th Street, tel: 212-265-6063; 1271 Broadway at 32nd Street, tel: 212-679-4365; Plaza Hotel, Central Park South, tel: 212-644-8264; and a Downtown office, 30 Vesey Street, tel: 212-227-8156.

Check www.amextravelresources. com for travel agencies that can provide American Express travelers check services. These include Up and Away Travel, 347 Fifth Avenue, tel: 212-889-2345.

Citibank offers exchange facilities at most branches; tel: 800-285-3000.

Refunds

Department stores usually allow you to return merchandise up to 30 days after purchase for full credit. Boutiques are less accommodating; some allow store credit only, no returns on sale items, and no returns or exchanges after seven days.

P

Postal services

Manhattan's main post office is on Eighth Avenue between 31st and 33rd streets; it is open 24 hours a day. To locate post offices elsewhere in the five boroughs, call 800-275-8777 or go to www.usps.com.

R

Religion

New York is approximately 60 percent Christian, 7 percent Jewish, 2 percent Muslim, and 5 percent agnostic, with Buddhists, Hindus, and others also represented. Some 6,000 churches, synagogues, temples, and mosques can be found in the city's five boroughs.

Rest stops

When energy flags, New York has thoughtfully provided seating areas on Broadway between 42nd and 47th streets, at Herald Square between 33rd and 35th streets, and around Lincoln Center. Public restrooms are found in public parks but otherwise are in short supply in New York. Look for department stores, hotels, large book stores, or Starbucks coffee shops, which do have restrooms. In some cases you will have to request a key.

S

Security

Be prepared to pass through security checkpoints with metal detectors at such tourist attractions as the Statue of Liberty and Empire State Building.

Traffic in Chelsea

Smoking

There is a no-smoking law in effect in virtually all New York City bars, restaurants, and offices. Be sure to request a smoking room if needed when booking a place to stay. The legal age to buy cigarettes is 21.

Street grid

In Midtown and Uptown Manhattan, avenues run north and south; streets run east and west. Even-numbered streets tend to have one-way eastbound traffic; odd-numbered streets, westbound traffic. Exceptions are 14th, 23rd, 57th, 72nd, 79th, and 86th streets, which have two-way traffic and crosstown bus services. Most avenues are one-way, except for Park Avenue which has two-way traffic north of 44th Street, and Broadway north of 57th Street. The picture is more confusing in Greenwich Village and other Downtown neighborhoods, where most streets have names instead of numbers and run at all angles.

T

Taxis

Taxis, all metered, cruise the streets and must be hailed, although there are designated taxi stands at bus and train stations. Be sure to flag down an official yellow cab. The light on top is lit when the cab is available. The base rate on taxi fares is $3.30 upon entry plus 50¢ for every one-fifth of a mile (when the taxicab is traveling at 6 miles an hour or more) or 60 seconds (when not in motion). The flat rate for a taxi between JFK and Manhattan is $52 plus tolls, with a $4.50 surcharge at peak times. There is a $1 surcharge on all taxi rides from 4pm to 8pm on weekdays, and a 50¢ surcharge from 8pm to 6am. Apps like Lyft and Uber have thousands of cars in New York – they are now said to outnumber official yellow taxis by 4 to 1.
24-hr taxi hotline: tel: 311

Water taxis

New York Water Taxis provide ferry service on the Hudson and East rivers. In addition to commuter services, water taxis offer hop-on-hop-off tours around the harbor on summer weekends and scenic tours. See www.nywatertaxi.com.

Telephone and faxes

Most Manhattan locations have a 212 area code, or the recently added 646 and 332. Cell phones can be 646 or 917. Brooklyn, Queens, Staten Island, and Bronx numbers are prefixed by 718 or the newer 347 and 929. The area code of the number being called must be used even within the city.

Toll-free calls are prefixed by 800, 866, 877, or 888.

Public telephones accepting credit cards are becoming scarce, but can still

be found in centers such as Grand Central Terminal and Penn Station. Hotels usually add a hefty surcharge for phone calls. Telephone dialing cards, available at convenience stores and newsstands, are an inexpensive way to make calls.

Cell phones

If you are a foreign traveler and your cell phone plan doesn't include international service, consider purchasing a prepaid cell phone or SIM card, available at most electronic stores.

Useful numbers

International calls, dial 011 (the international access code), then the country code, city code, and local number.
Directory help, dial 555-1212 preceded by the area code you are calling from, or 411.

Non-emergency services

New York has a three-digit number to be dialed for information and non-emergency services. Calls to 311 are answered by a live operator 24 hours a day, seven days a week, and services are provided in over 170 languages. Operators are prepared to respond to a wide range of calls, including tourist inquiries, complaints about noise, queries about public transportation, and information about lost items.

Time zone

New York observes Eastern Standard Time (EST) and Eastern Daylight Time (EDT). This is usually five hours behind London, and always one hour ahead of Chicago, and three hours ahead of California.

Tipping

Most New Yorkers in the service industries (restaurants, hotels, transportation) regard tips as a God-given right, not just a pleasant gratuity. The fact is, many people rely on tips to make up for what are often poor hourly salaries. Therefore, unless service is truly horrendous, you can figure on tipping everyone from bellmen and porters (usually $1 a bag; or $2 if only one bag); to hotel doormen ($2 if they hail you a cab); hotel maids ($1–2 a day, left in your room when you check out), rest-room attendants (at least 50¢), and room-service waiters (approximately 15 percent of the bill unless already added on). In restaurants, an easy way to figure out the tip is to double the tax, which adds up to a little more than 16 percent (though 18–20 percent is becoming standard). In taxis, tip 15 percent of the total fare.

Tourist information

Official New York City Information Center: Macy's Herald Sqaure 151 W. 34th Street (between Seventh Avenue and Broadway); tel: 212-484-1200, 800-NYC-VISIT; www.nycgo.com; Mon–Fri 9am–7pm, Sat 10am–7pm, Sun 11am–7pm. The center offers brochures, maps, and information about hotels and attraction discounts.

Brooklyn Bridge

Transportation

Subways and buses

Subways and buses run 24 hours a day, less frequently (and some lines not at all) after midnight. Fares are payable by MetroCard pass (available at subway ticket booths), which allows free transfers between buses or buses and subways within two hours of use. Unlimited-ride passes for seven or 30 days are available.

Buses run on most avenues (except Park Avenue) as well as on the following cross-streets: Houston, 14th, 23rd, 34th, 42nd, 49th–50th, 57th, 66th, 79th, 86th, 96th, 116th, and 125th.

Subway shuttle trains cross town at 14th and 42nd streets. Queens lines N and R also cross from east to west in Manhattan. There is no north–south line east of Lexington Avenue or west of Eighth Avenue and Broadway.

For bus and subway information, call: 718-330-1234 or 511, or see www.mta.info.

PATH trains

PATH (Port Authority Trans Hudson) trains run under the Hudson River from Manhattan to Hoboken, Jersey City, and Newark in New Jersey. For information, call 800-234-PATH, or see www.panynj.gov/path.

Rail and bus stations

Long-distance and commuter trains arrive and depart from Manhattan's Grand Central Terminal at Park Avenue and 42nd Street, and Pennsylvania Station at Seventh Avenue and 33rd Street. For information on Amtrak, the national rail service, tel: 800-872-7245, www.amtrak.com.

The city's main bus terminal is Port Authority (625 Eighth Avenue between 40th and 42nd streets). The station sits on two subway lines and is serviced by long-distance bus companies (including Greyhound: tel: 800-231-2222; www.greyhound.com) and commuter lines. City buses stop outside.

W

Websites

www.citysearch.com/guide/newyork-ny-metro for listings and reviews of current arts and entertainment events, as well as restaurants and shopping.

www.nyc.gov is the official site of the City of New York.

www.nycgo.com is the New York City tourism website, with information on hotels, restaurants, shopping, events, and promotions.

www.centralparknyc.org details what's on at and all about Central Park, including maps.

http://ny.eater.com reviews of the hottest New York restaurants and eateries.

www.nypl.org is for everything you ever wanted to know about the New York Public Library. There's also an online information service.

Weights and measures

The US uses the imperial system.

The 'Sex and the City' ladies

BOOKS AND FILM

The year 1888, when writer William Dean Howells abandoned Boston for the Big Apple, is often seen as the moment when New York moved into the lead of America's literary enterprise. And so it remains. The industry nurtured such major talents as Henry James and Edith Wharton, who forged an old New York mystique later augmented by waves of writers coming from other cultures – Jewish, Irish, African-American, Italian, and more.

When it comes to movies, there's something about New York that loves the camera. From all those wide-angle sweeps up, down, and across the city's imposing skyscrapers to the down-and-dirty peeks at what lies beneath, movie-makers have found Gotham an irresistible backdrop.

Books

History

The Gangs of New York: An Informal History of the Underworld by Herbert Asbury. The book on which the Martin Scorsese film is based takes readers on a journey to a bygone New York, when violent gangs ruled the Five Points near present-day City Hall.

Gotham: A History of New York to 1898 by Mike Wallace and Edwin G. Burrows. Pulitzer Prize-winning narrative about the city's early years; in-depth, with an emphasis on some of its characters.

How the Other Half Lives by Jacob Riis. Groundbreaking account of the squalid tenements and sweatshops of the 19th century.

New York: The Story of a Great City edited by Sarah Henry. A concise, visual history of the city as compiled by the Museum of the City of New York.

Writing New York: A Literary Anthology edited by Philip Lopate. Observations about life in New York by such literary folk as Henry David Thoreau, Walt Whitman, Maxim Gorky, and F. Scott Fitzgerald.

Contemporary non-fiction

New York Stories: The Best of the City Section of the New York Times edited by Constance Rosenblum. An anthology of essays about city life from the Times.

The Nanny Diaries by Emma McLaughlin and Nicola Kraus. A fascinating insight into the cruel world of Manhattan's upper crust.

Sex and the City by Candace Bushnell. These sex columns from the New York Observer served as the inspiration for the popular TV series.

Still Life in Harlem by Eddy L. Harris. An autobiographical take on this storied African-American neighborhood.

Fiction

The Age of Innocence by Edith Wharton. A portrait of upper-crust New York in the 19th century.

Gene Hackman takes notes in 'The French Connection'

The Catcher in the Rye by J.D. Salinger. A masterpiece that perfectly captures New York in the '50s.

The Bonfire of the Vanities by Tom Wolfe. Satirical novel set in the New York of the 1980s.

Bright Lights, Big City by Jay McInerney. Novel set in yuppie New York during the cocaine-saturated 1980s by one of the period's rising literary stars.

Wonderful Town: New York Stories from The New Yorker edited by David Remnick. Work by Philip Roth, John Cheever, Susan Sontag, and others are collected in this anthology of short stories from the venerable literary magazine.

Films

Here's just a short selection of iconic New York movies.

Miracle on 34th Street, 1947. A classic Christmas story. The 1994 remake is even more sugary than the original, but Richard Attenborough makes a good Santa Claus.

Breakfast at Tiffany's, 1961. Audrey Hepburn and George Peppard search for love, diamonds, and breakfast in a bittersweet tale based (with some huge liberties taken) on the Truman Capote novel.

West Side Story, 1961. Romeo and Juliet are transported to Hell's Kitchen with irresistible energy in this near-definitive New York musical by Leonard Bernstein and Stephen Sondheim.

Midnight Cowboy, 1969. Dustin Hoffman and Jon Voight are down-on-their-luck hustlers in this vivid evocation of 1960s street life.

The French Connection, 1971. A riveting performance by Gene Hackman as cop Popeye Doyle, and the daddy of all New York car chases.

Taxi Driver, 1976. Martin Scorsese directs Robert De Niro as a psychotic cabbie who tries to save a child prostitute played by Jodie Foster.

Wall Street, 1987. 'Greed is good,' declares Michael Douglas in this Oliver Stone film, neatly summing up the excesses of the go-go 1980s.

Manhattan, 1979. Woody Allen's ode to his hometown and his own neuroses is shot in black and white and stars Allen, Diane Keaton, and Meryl Streep.

Do the Right Thing, 1989. Spike Lee riffs on racial tensions in Brooklyn's Bedford-Stuyvesant neighborhood.

When Harry Met Sally, 1989. The city looks fantastic in this romantic comedy about friendship and love, with Meg Ryan and Billy Crystal.

Nick and Norah's Infinite Playlist, 2008. A coming-of-age romantic comedy in the world of indie rock which takes place in one evening mostly in the Lower East Side and East Village.

The Avengers, 2012. The metropolis ends up a little worse-for-wear after this superhero extravaganza.

Whiplash, 2014. The story of a complicated relationship between an ambitious jazz student and his abusive instructor at a prestigious New York music school.

The Big Short, 2015. Christian Bale and Brad Pitt star in this entertaining take on the financial crisis of 2007–8.

ABOUT THIS BOOK

This *Explore Guide* has been produced by the editors of Insight Guides, whose books have set the standard for visual travel guides since 1970. With top-quality photography and authoritative recommendations, these guidebooks bring you the very best routes and itineraries in the world's most exciting destinations.

BEST ROUTES

The routes in the book provide something to suit all budgets, tastes and trip lengths. As well as covering the destination's many classic attractions, the itineraries track lesser-known sights. The routes embrace a range of interests, so whether you are an art fan, a gourmet, a history buff or have kids to entertain, you will find an option to suit.

We recommend reading the whole of a route before setting out. This should help you to familiarise yourself with it and enable you to plan where to stop for refreshments – options are shown in the 'Food and Drink' box at the end of each tour.

For our pick of the tours by theme, consult Recommended Routes for... (see pages 6–7).

INTRODUCTION

The routes are set in context by this introductory section, giving an overview of the destination to set the scene, plus background information on food and drink, shopping and more, while a succinct history timeline highlights the key events over the centuries.

DIRECTORY

Also supporting the routes is a Directory chapter, with a clearly organised A–Z of practical information, our pick of where to stay while you are there and select restaurant listings; these eateries complement the more low-key cafés and restaurants that feature within the routes and are intended to offer a wider choice for evening dining. Also included here are some nightlife listings and our recommendations for books and films about the destination.

ABOUT THE AUTHORS

Writer Aaron Starmer has spent the last twelve years exploring the streets, parks, and restaurants of New York City. He has written and contributed to numerous guidebooks, including *Insight City Guide New York*, and is the author of two novels for young people.

This new edition was thoroughly updated by Dan Stables and draws on original content by Eleanor Berman and John Gattuso, as well as Edward A. Jardim, William Scheller, Kathy Novak, and Divya Symmers.

CONTACT THE EDITORS

We hope you find this Explore Guide useful, interesting and a pleasure to read. If you have any questions or feedback on the text, pictures or maps, please do let us know. If you have noticed any errors or outdated facts, or have suggestions for places to include on the routes, we would be delighted to hear from you. Please drop us an email at hello@insightguides.com. Thanks!

CREDITS

Explore New York
Editor: Sian Marsh
Author: Aaron Starmer, Eleanor Berman,
John Gattuso
Head of DTP and Pre-Press: Rebeka Davies
Updated By: Dan Stables
Managing Editor: Carine Tracanelli
Picture Editor: Tom Smyth
Cartography: original cartography
Berndtson & Berndtson, updated by Carte
Photo credits: Ace Hotels 109; Alamy 22, 23,
123, 136; AWL Images 1, 4/5T, 26/27T; Bel-
mond 118/119; Bigstock 72, 88/89, 100/101;
Britta Jaschinski/Apa Publications 4MC, 20,
21L, 28/29, 29L, 31, 62, 64, 64/65, 65L, 66,
68, 80/81, 81L, 87, 88, 96, 97, 101L, 120; Casablanca Hotel 104; Daniel 115L; Dreamstime
4MR, 6TL, 6BC, 11T, 28, 36, 40, 40/41, 48, 49L,
50, 50/51, 51L, 52, 52/53, 57L, 61, 63L, 78,
78/79, 94/95, 98, 124, 128/129; Fotolia 4MR,
8ML, 26MC, 62/63, 70/71, 116/117; Getty
Images 6ML, 58, 122, 125L, 137; Gramercy
Tavern 102ML; iStock 4MC, 4ML, 7MR, 7M,
7MR, 10, 10/11T, 26ML, 26ML, 26MR, 32, 33L,
34, 36/37, 37L, 38, 42/43, 44, 44/45, 47,
48/49, 54, 57B, 60, 73, 76, 83, 84, 92, 98/99,
99L, 100, 102MR, 102/103T; Keiko Niwa/Lower
East Side Tenement Museum 91; Leonardo
102MR, 105, 106, 106/107, 107L, 110, 111,
114; ; Mary Evans Picture Library 24, 25; Michael Bodycomb/The Frick Collection 59; Nowitz
Photography/Apa Publications 4ML, 6MC, 8ML,
8MC, 8MC, 8MR, 8MR, 8/9T, 10/11M, 12,
12/13, 13L, 14T, 14B, 15, 17T, 17B, 18, 19,
20/21, 26MR, 26MC, 30, 32/33, 35, 45L, 46,
53L, 55, 56, 56/57, 67, 68/69, 69L, 74, 75,
77, 79L, 80, 82, 85, 86, 89L, 90, 92/93, 93L,
102MC, 121, 124/125, 126, 126/127, 127L,
130, 130/131, 131L, 132, 133, 134/135; Paul
Kolnik/New York City Ballet 7T; Robert Harding
39, 41L; Shutterstock 113; Starwood Hotels &
Resorts 108, 112; Stephen Beaudet 102MC;
The Standard 102ML; Thomas Schauer/Daniel
16, 114/115
Cover credits: Antonino Bartucci-
o/4Corners Images (main) iStock (bottom)

DISTRIBUTION

UK, Ireland and Europe
Apa Publications (UK) Ltd
sales@insightguides.com
United States and Canada
Ingram Publisher Services
ips@ingramcontent.com
Australia and New Zealand
Woodslane
info@woodslane.com.au
Southeast Asia
Apa Publications (Singapore) Pte
singaporeoffice@insightguides.com
Worldwide
Apa Publications (UK) Ltd
sales@insightguides.com

SPECIAL SALES, CONTENT LICENSING AND COPUBLISHING

Insight Guides can be purchased in bulk
quantities at discounted prices. We can
create special editions, personalised jackets
and corporate imprints tailored to your needs.
sales@insightguides.com
www.insightguides.biz

INDEX

MAP LEGEND

●   Start of tour

⇥   Tour & route direction

❶   Recommended sight

❷   Recommended restaurant/café

★   Place of interest
ⓘ   Tourist information
Ⓜ   Subway station
⚲   Statue/monument
✉   Main post office
🚌   Main bus station
----   Ferry route
━ ━   National park boundry
·---   District boundary

   Park
   Important building
   Hotel
   Transport hub
   Shopping / mall
   Pedestrian area
   Urban area
   Marsh